Little Farm
in the Foothills

A Boomer Couple's
Search for the Slow Life

Susan Colleen Browne

with John F. Browne

Whitethorn Press

Whitethorn Press
Bellingham, Washington

In memory of my father,
James Willis Davis

and

Robin

Acknowledgments

Heartfelt thanks to the early readers of this book, Lori Nelson-Clonts, Patty Kelly, and Becky Burns, for your encouragement, critical eyes and insightful suggestions. Many thanks as well to Patricia Davis, champion editor and proofreader, and Kate Weisel, pre-press wizard. We are eternally grateful to our children Sasha, Collin, Carrie and Meghann for their love and support. Sasha, your helpful feedback on cover layout, and Meghann, your logo design, was especially appreciated!

Although they are no longer with us, we are indebted to our beloved fathers James Davis and Sid Browne for their lifelong lessons and inspiration. Finally, we owe a tremendous debt of gratitude to Nanette Davis and Burl Harmon for providing "shelter from the storm." Without you, Berryridge Farm would still be only a dream.

PART I

"Do not go where the path may lead, go instead where there is no path and leave a trail."

—Ralph Waldo Emerson

1 🦋 Seeking Walden

It's said that if you want to figure out your life's passion, look at what you loved as a child. When I was growing up, I loved Barbies. You might think, there's a girl who'll go far, what with Astronaut Barbie and Internist Barbie and Professional Figure Skater Barbie. Actually, I predate all those ambitious, take-the-world-by-the-horns Barbies. In *my* time, back in the sixties, all Barbie did was sit around and look hot and wait for Ken to ask her out.

But I also loved to read, especially fairy tales like Sleeping Beauty, and stories about gutsy, courageous girls like Jo March and Laura Ingalls. And when I wasn't reading or hanging out with Barbie, Midge, and Skipper, I was playing in the woods behind our house. Maybe I was living out fantasies inspired by Sleeping Beauty's forest hideaway, or Laura's "Little House" series, but I found my bliss climbing trees, building forts and riding my bike around Woodland Hills, a new development perched on the rural edge of St. Cloud, Minnesota.

My husband, John, was an outdoorsy kid too, with a childhood a lot like mine. (Minus the Barbies.) Your mother sent you outside to play after breakfast, and except for lunch, you were supposed to stay there until it got dark or dinnertime, whichever came first. But then, you didn't really want to be indoors anyway. Certainly not John—from what I can tell, he *lived* "The Dangerous Book for Boys." He'd roam nearby woods and fields with his little gang of friends, playing Robin Hood or cowboys and Indians, coming home so dirty his mom would have to hose him down.

Later, as a young husband and father, John got his fresh air nurturing a small vegetable plot for his family. But it could be the outdoor activities so many of us love as adults, like camping, hiking, and gardening—and I hear vacations on working farms are getting popular!—are a way to free our inner tree-climbing, mud-lovin' child. To return to a simpler time, when most people lived on farms—or at least *knew* a farmer. A time when you spent far more of your life outside than in.

Whatever it is, I never stopped loving the outdoors, and John never lost his longing for wide open spaces...a love and longing we indulged with our mutual passion for gardening. But there came a time when we both yearned for a deeper connection with the land...for a more peaceful life, one more attuned to nature's pace. Okay, that sounds pretty highfalutin'—all we *thought* we wanted was more room for a kitchen garden, and a little quiet in which to enjoy it. Regardless of our goal, our journey to that life began the day we reached our tipping point with urban noise and traffic and crowds...when John and I bucked our play-it-safe, risk-averse natures and decided to leave the city. *Little Farm in the Foothills* is the tale of our fifty-something leap of faith, to seek out a slower, simpler, and more serene lifestyle on a rural acreage. And embrace a whole new way of living.

Who'd have guessed how complicated "simplicity" could get. Or that serenity and reinventing your life was no match made in heaven.

Before I hit my Boomer years, I'd never seriously considered living in the country.

Despite my woods-playing, I hadn't spent much time in the true boondocks. In elementary school, I'd been a Campfire Girl, but my group never went camping or sat around a campfire—much less lit one. I'd gone tent camping exactly once in my life, a post-high school girlfriend getaway memorable only for the fact that for the entire three days, we'd frozen our eighteen-year-old tushies off. In June!

Anyhow, I'm all for city comforts. Call me picky (I'm the first to admit I'm annoyingly germ-conscious), but I'd always been sort of revolted by the idea of an on-site septic system. There's all that "stuff" in a tank right next to your house, for Pete's sake. And I liked city

water. The only well water I'd tasted was loaded with sulfurous compounds, and the rotten-egg smell wafting up from your glass would
set off a gag reflex. I didn't want water from just *anywhere*—it could
be unhygienic, okay? I have a B.S. in environmental studies. I *know*
about contaminated groundwater. I wanted my drinking water from
nice clean municipal water treatment plants.

But water was only a side issue. In my youth, I'd had the kind of
country experience that would turn most people off permanently.

2 ❦ Down(er) on the Farm

My brief fling with rural living was not, as Jane Austen would
put it, felicitous. My first husband had been a farm boy, and
had worked all through high school at a neighbor's operation, milking cows and making silage. After Terry graduated, though, he was
done with farming—he planned a career in a technical field instead
of a cornfield. But the third year of our marriage, when he was
languishing in college after a stint in the Navy, he had a change of
heart. One November day, Terry decided that country life would be
a great way to recharge his batteries, and took a job as a milker on
a large dairy farm.

As a young mom with a toddler, I suppose I was game for a new
adventure. The night before the job started, we were invited to our
new boss' home for cherry pie. I took in the Van H.'s cozy farmhouse,
with the gingham tablecloth and colonial-style maple furniture, and
smiled at Mrs. Van H., thinking, *this could be fun*. Then again, it
could've been the yummy pie...but still.

My smile lasted right up until I walked into our new home. Farm
employees, you see, are often supplied with a place to live. Our on-
site residence, near the milking parlor, was a beat-up single-wide
trailer that should give you new sympathy for the housing plight of
seasonal farm workers.

The Van H. farmhouse was about a quarter-mile from the farm,
while the mobile, I kid you not, was sitting right next to, and I do
mean practically right on top of, the cow pen adjacent to the barn.
This place was the filthiest dwelling I'd ever moved into. Grime and

mouse droppings everywhere. And you understand I was more germ-conscious than most people. Probably more germ-conscious than most bacteriologists. Farmer Van H. was of Dutch descent, and though I hate to perpetuate ethnic stereotypes, aren't the Dutch supposed to be big on cleanliness being next to godliness? For a year, my sister had lived in The Netherlands, and told me how those tidy Dutch homemakers kept their homes spotless. They even swept and washed the front steps each day. "Clean" was their middle name. Well, this guy was the exception to the rule.

Although my days were full already with Carrie, our fifteen month-old baby, and doing a newspaper motor route I shared with hubby, I embarked on Project Mobile Muck-Out. Every fixture and appliance, every cupboard, windowsill and inch of floor had to be wiped down and sanitized. I was a whirling dervish, a younger, poorer Martha Stewart on a mission.

Around midnight of the third day, I stripped off my well-worn rubber gloves, and gazed around with satisfaction. With my house clean, the mice droppings only a memory, I felt like a whole new woman. Life was back on track.

Or so I thought.

Here in Western Washington, the prevailing air mass off the Pacific Ocean means it never gets all that cold—mostly in the forties, even in the middle of winter. This being the case, apparently Farmer Van H. felt that certain house amenities were an option instead of a require-ment. Like insulation. The mobile had no skirting beneath it, or other protection from the elements. We had to keep the electric furnace going day and night, and the place was still frigid. Not surprisingly, our first electric bill exceeded a month's worth of groceries.

Despite the trailer's inadequate underpinning, I figured that since I hadn't seen any mice in the house, there weren't any. My blissful ignorance didn't last long. One evening, alone with Carrie, I settled her into her highchair for dinner. I opened a cupboard to get out a package of pasta and out jumped a mouse. It landed on my thigh and scampered down my leg.

"Aacckk," I screamed, leaping back. Shuddering in revulsion, I screeched again, then glanced at the baby. She promptly burst into tears. I managed to pull myself together—despite the sensation of mouse feet lingering on my leg—comforted Carrie, then examined my food supplies. The mouse had been munching on our lone loaf of bread, and the pasta package had holes in it. So, this loathsome species could actually *eat* through plastic bags. Out went the bread, and on my next trip to town, I had to spend some of our meager grocery money on two sturdy Rubbermaid bins for food storage.

Strapping my rubber gloves back on, I resumed my search for mouse droppings. Not only did I have a freezing house next to a cow pen, I had to share it with mice.

3 🦋 Thank God
I'm (Not) a Country Girl

Now that I was unofficially a farmer's wife, I had to adjust to a different kind of lifestyle, which included a more cavalier attitude toward living things. One day, outside the milking parlor, I found a dead calf. Now, I know "stuff happens." But did Mr. Van H. (who shall otherwise remain unnamed) need to leave this poor little dead thing lying out in the open for three days?

Farm life was also more isolating than I'd counted on. Being a full-time mommy, I had to forgo the bicycling I'd always enjoyed, so for fresh air, I'd take Carrie for a stroller ride each day. But here on the farm, walking was out too—with the nearest town about eight miles away, the only accessible road was the busy highway fronting our humble abode. I could hardly take my baby for a jaunt on the road shoulder while double-trailer semis roared by.

One day, desperate to exercise, I packed Carrie into her baby-backpack, hoisted her onto my shoulders, and ventured into the denuded cornfield next to the dairy barn. About halfway across the field, I met our boss, Farmer Van H. "Out for a walk, are you?" he said with a chuckle.

"That's right," I said, smiling. Okay, he'd housed us in pigsty, but other than that he was a really nice guy. "This break in the rain won't last long."

"You know, I just painted the field," said he, with another *hee, hee.*

I kept smiling. Painted the field? "That's okay. I really want a walk."

Well, there's one good thing about winter in the country: the cold sort of covers up dairy farm smells. It took me about a quarter mile of hiking to figure out what he meant by "painted." He'd just spread manure all over the field, manure that now covered my lone pair of sneakers. And the only way home was to retrace my steps through the cowpie-laden field again.

My one opportunity for a change of scenery was my part-time job delivering newspapers. It wasn't exactly dinner out on the town, or even a trip to the library. But for a few hours, ensconced in our little Nissan, I could get away from that beastly trailer.

Driving a motor route isn't the mindless activity you might imagine. It's not just a talent, but an art form, shooting a rolled-up paper into a square plastic tube, calculating how hard to brake so you can hit your target and still keep your car moving. For entertainment, I had two cassette tapes (remember those?), a Haydn trumpet concerto and one of Gerry Rafferty's, the '70's popmeister. Driving along country roads, I'd crank up "Baker Street," and sing along with some guy's dream about buying land, and giving up booze and one-night stands. I had minimal experience with booze, and none with one-night-stands, but at twenty-three, with a husband and baby, I reveled in my temporary freedom. Taking in the beauty of the Cascade Foothills around me, ringing our county's farms and fields, I inhaled the brisk—albeit manure-scented—air drifting into the car. Despite our crummy digs, at moments like these, I could say life was pretty darn good.

Then real winter set in.

Once or twice each season, our mild winters take a holiday when northeast winds sweep down from the Canadian prairies. This easterly flow pushes aside the marine air, and brings bitter cold. And a local geographical quirk ensures that there's no escaping this wintry blast: a river valley to the north funnels that biting wind straight into our county, especially the flat farmlands. When you're used to forty degrees Fahrenheit, the wind chill of these northeasters steals your breath.

One January day on the Van H. farm, a northeaster blew in. A bummer, since our electric bill would go from painful to through the roof, but certainly no tragedy. But in our under-insulated home-sweet-home, something more sinister was at work than a little cold air: by day's end, our plumbing froze solid. And how could this happen so fast, you might ask? Another feature of the trailer was that the wastewater exited our place via an unwrapped pipe. You might think Farmer Van H. was unaware of this arrangement, except this unprotected pipe was clearly visible from every direction.

Later that night, the plumbing backed up into the toilet and bathtub. The boss turned out to be as cavalier about housing repairs as dead livestock removal. After three days of hiking up to the milking parlor to use the facilities inside (when it was unlocked, that is), or being reduced to peeing in a five-gallon bucket in a freezing, sewage-filled bathroom while Farmer Van H. ignored our phone calls, I put my foot—in its manure-stained sneaker—down. "Terry," I said to my husband, "we're leaving."

He felt badly about ditching Mr. Van H., but at that point, he could choose his boss, or his family. He chose wisely. After I'd packed up our things, I left the farm and country life without a backward look. Maybe I wasn't exactly scarred for life, but I came away with enough Post-Sewage Stress Syndrome to dream about backed-up toilets for months.

Me, even *entertain* the notion of moving back to the country? No. Way.

4 ❧ City Livin'

What a difference a couple of decades can make. I was newly married to John, and we'd recently bought a just-finished, spanking clean home (with no mice) in a community we loved: Bellingham, Washington. A college town in a jewel of a natural setting, Bellingham is an artistic, educational, and recreational mecca with a laid-back, counterculture energy. As a middle-of-the-road type, part buttoned-up traditionalist, part free-and-easy non-conformist, I'd loved this town from my first visit back in 1975.

Our house was located on a quiet, scenic little block the builders called the "Street of Dreams." This was a huge stretch, given the modest size and design of the homes (nothing like the bazillion-dollar dwellings in most "Street of Dreams" developments), but with the surrounding greenbelts and open space, we were happy to play along with their fantasy.

John had been a good sport about buying in town, when in fact, his dream was to have a country spread. In his twenties, he'd come close to realizing his heart's desire, when he and his first wife purchased ten acres outside of town. If anyone was made for country living, it was John.

"I'm a dirt guy," says John.

I always have been. When I was three years old, back in Wichita, Kansas, one morning my mother got me dressed, combed my hair, and sent me out to play. As Mom tells it, I came back a few minutes later bare-naked, dirty water dripping off my head. "What have you been up to, young man?" she asked.

"I shampooed my hair," I said proudly.

She sighed resignedly. "And where did you do that?"

"In a mud puddle!" I didn't get a spanking, but I did get my hair washed. Twice.

A few years later, the city waterworks department dug a couple of drainage ditches near our house. My buddies and I would charge over to play our version of trench warfare, using dirt clods for grenades. I'd just turned nine when my family moved to Bellevue, Washington, and was still big on mud. We lived near a small lake, and one day, exploring the swampy shallows, I discovered a clutch of polliwogs—frogs that look like part fish, when they've grown little legs but haven't lost their tails yet. I was determined to collect a bunch, but I didn't have anything to carry them in. So I stretched my tee-shirt into a bowl and headed home with a dozen or so polliwogs cradled in my shirt, squirming next to my stomach.

When I went off to college, I put my love of mud to good use. I majored in dirt—also known as ceramics. Toiling happily with wet clay every day, I could even call it art. And during all those hours in the ceramics studio, I could be a kid again.

Clearly, John hadn't changed much from his nature boy days. What else is ceramics than mud pies for grown-ups?

By the late 1970s, John's ceramics days were behind him. With his newly purchased property, he had an acreage to tame, and a place for his little son and daughter to play. A full-time police officer, John was eager to spend his off-hours planting an orchard and a big vegetable garden. He and his wife were in the process of choosing house floor plans when the marriage unexpectedly broke up. His wife got the house, John the acreage, and soon after, he reluctantly sold it to start a small retirement fund. His dream, sadly, was not to be.

Now, in our new home, John made up for the urban setting by creating a little haven in our backyard. As dedicated homebodies, we filled it with berry plants, herbs, and fruit trees, with space for tomatoes, zucchini, and sugar snap peas…and flowers. Hyacinths blossomed in April, Siberian iris in May, and stargazer lilies in June. The bee balm, hardy fuchsia, and one perfect rosebush bloomed all summer long, accented by the stone fountain John had designed and installed. Our garden was an oasis of tranquility, where, on summer weekends, I'd take my morning tea to sit under John's hand-crafted arbor, shaded by grapevines entwined through the trellis overhead. Nights, I'd pop outside for stargazing, and maybe catch a meteor or two. At my luckiest, in late fall, I'd get a panoramic view of the aurora borealis.

If we had one minor glitch in our private little Eden, it was the household next door. Elsie, an older lady with a soft southern drawl, was a real sweetheart. She loved everybody. She also loved dogs. She loved them so much she had five of them, matching white-pink toy poodles she called "my little darlins.'" Elsie had installed a convenient doggie-door so this poodle quintet was free to go outside at will, and their lone entertainment was to run into the backyard and yap at anything that moved. Passersby, neighbor kids playing, and the two of us, working in our garden, were fair game. What kept John and me from going nuts was that with a stern word (or three) from Elsie, her darlins' would stop barking, and peace would once again reign supreme.

Then our neighborhood began to expand.

5 ❦ Urban Nightmare

The trees surrounding our vicinity began to disappear as new cul-de-sacs were carved out of the woods, new homes popping up like mushrooms in fall. Our small city started a growth spurt too, getting as leggy as a fourteen-year-old boy. But one spring day, just when we figured our neighborhood had *finally* run out of growing space, there came another inescapable portent of change.

Two pretty young women showed up at our door with a plate of perfectly-baked chocolate chip cookies. Obviously college kids, they'd just moved into the house kitty-corner to ours. *How sweet*, I thought as I thanked them. I guess they didn't realize it's the other way around—that people *already* living in the neighborhood are supposed to bring goodies to the new folks—but for all their youth, they already seemed like the perfect neighbors.

Then a second kitty-corner house sold. The block suddenly acquired five more college kids. With six cars crowding the driveway.

Dismayed, John and I kvetched to each other, "Is this legal?" It must have been, because as the months passed, more and more homes on our street turned into college rentals. Volkswagen Jettas and dual-exhaust Hondas vroomed up the street, sub-woofers thumping. Stereos boomed from open windows, and weekend parties often lasted until 2 a.m. How long would it be, we asked ourselves, before ours was the sole owner-occupied home in the area?

And just like neighborhoods change, so do neighbors—like sweet old Elsie next door. Her grown daughter had moved in with her, and they turned out to be quite a tempestuous pair. Lots of bickering and arguments, all conducted at the top of their lungs. Then Elsie became chronically ill, and the daughter her reluctant caretaker. As

Mom's illness worsened, so did the fights—just in time for the warm weather. And with the windows open, we heard them all.

That summer, nature seemed to be working against us. The lush backyard garden we'd created by hand, the trees and berries and flowers we'd loved and cosseted, began to go downhill. Like us, had they just had enough? The pear trees were rife with fungus. The frost peaches shriveled on the tree. The blueberry crop plummeted. The tomatoes and beans languished. The robins beat us to the grapes and cleaned them out. Frankly, our plants seemed as miserable as we were.

Less than a mile away, the city finished a new athletic complex, with acres of playing fields. Nighttime soccer games now played almost year-round, so the light pollution was immense. Instead of the moon illuminating the night sky, it was skyscraper-high field lights. The celestial events I'd enjoyed had been all but obliterated.

The noise intensified. A line of tall Douglas firs between our street and the interstate were felled for more houses, and with the natural sound barrier gone, the roar of the freeway added to the commotion. Neighbors began hiring out their lawn care, and soon commercial-grade, designed-for-speed mowers, weed-eaters, and leaf-blowers drowned out the morning birdsong. Yet another neighbor behind us embarked on what seemed to be a permanent home improvement regime. Sunup to sundown, his tractor grumbled and power-washer whined. More roads and housing projects brought construction vehicles of every stripe rumbling up and down our previously peaceful lane.

That same summer, a single mom and her ten-year-old son moved in directly across the street. They were a delightful twosome: she was a hands-on mom, and the boy was unusually well-mannered. The rub? He loved to skateboard. Mom had let him construct a skateboard jump in front of the garage, and each day, for hours, unless it was actively snowing, he'd be on that jump. Rattle, rattle, rattle, ker*thump*! Rattle, rattle, rattle, ker*thump*! Rattle, rattle, rattle, kerTHUMP! The boy had lots of friends too, who seemed to spend all their spare time at his house. Doing what, you may ask? Skateboarding, of course. After a few hours, your ears would ring, but there was no respite. Rattle, rattle, rattle, *KERTHUMP*!

All. Day. Long.

It wasn't just the neighborhood that had changed. Our city—the cute little kid who'd bulked up like a ballplayer on steroids—had been "discovered" by the outside world. Articles extolling its virtues appeared in the national media, like *The New York Times*, *Runner's World*, and *AARP Magazine*. Development all over town stepped up dramatically, big box stores squatting on what had been gently rolling wetlands; the charmingly funky historical district on the waterfront had turned into high-rise, view-blocking condo-land.

The whole mood of the city began to shift. Its counterculture, slow-pokey flavor had disappeared, replaced by crowded roads where running red lights and speeding became the rule, not the exception. Everyone seemed caught in an almighty, big city rush. This get-away-from-it-all town that many people wanted to move *to*, was now the place we wanted to move *from*.

Then Elsie took a turn for the worse, with a stroke and dementia. "Help me, help me," she'd keen. "I was just in there!" the beleaguered daughter would snap back. The neglected toy poodles, without guidance from their mistress, wandered disconsolately in their yard, yapping aimlessly. You could hardly poke your head out the door without being assaulted by the din. Craving quiet, John and I barricaded ourselves indoors. He stopped working in the garden. I did the minimum. Sadly, the plants responded in kind. And my greatest outdoor joy, drinking tea and puttering in the dappled garden we'd created, became only a memory.

We were trapped.

6 🌱 Ch-Changes

They say there are only two things you can count on: death and taxes. But once you hit your mid-forties, you can also plan on being stampeded by change. Your circle of family and friends is constantly in flux—an endless herd of births, graduations, and weddings; illnesses, relocations, and deaths.

You might find yourself in low spirits, mourning not only your dear ones, but your youth. Maybe even your former waistline. For women, there's the joy of perimenopause—not exactly the icing on your midlife cake. With this barrage of new dilemmas and dramas, life starts resembling nothing so much as a soap opera…the plot twists and turns making you feel like you're on a runaway train with no emergency brakes.

Our own midlife "Days of our Lives" began one chill November night when John developed a burning pressure in his chest. We were tempted to blame the extra-spicy chili he'd eaten for dinner. But as a longtime police sergeant who'd taught CPR, John had seen too many medical emergencies to downplay his own. Around nine o'clock, he sat on the stairs and looked up at me, rubbing his sternum. "I, uh, hate to tell you this, but the pain's going down my left arm too."

"Your *left* arm?" I echoed.

"I think you'd better take me to the hospital."

With my dad chronically ill following two massive coronaries, we'd seen up close how debilitating heart trouble could be. John's symptoms, then, were nothing to mess around with. Before you can say "chest pain," off we drove to the local hospital, where we discovered John was indeed having exactly what he'd suspected.

A heart attack.

I thought I was gonna die.

As I sat on an ER bed, Sue at my side, a nurse gave me a nitroglycerin tablet to put under my tongue. Within seconds, I felt myself slipping away—I really thought I was a goner. "I don't feel so good," I muttered. "I'm going to faint."

"There's something wrong with him!" Sue called to the staff.

A nurse stepped back to my bedside. "Oh, you need to lie down." Once I was prone, I woozily sensed people scurrying around me. When I opened my eyes, I found Sue gazing down at me, looking anxious. "I've never seen anyone go white like that," she said as they hooked me up to an EKG machine. "You really gave us a scare."

"Nitroglycerin opens up your blood vessels really fast," the nurse told us. "That's why you can faint." The lesson with nitro is that unlike life's trials and tribulations, you should always take it lying down.

Here's what else happens when you go into the ER with chest pains. Besides the usual IV, you're plugged into a blood pressure/pulse rate monitor. You also get your blood drawn every four hours or so to check for a certain protein in your system—a by-product produced by the death of heart muscle. That's how doctors can assess the severity of a heart attack.

The resident cardiologist told me my EKG looked pretty normal. "But to be safe," he said, "I'd like to schedule you for an angiogram in the morning." The procedure would check for heart blockages—that is, plaque build-up in your arteries. If the angiogram showed a problem, they would proceed with the proper treatment—and if I agreed, would I please sign this form.

What am I going to say, "No, just leave me to my fate?" I signed the form. The next morning I got the test results: my blood showed no evidence of heart muscle death. But I still had the angiogram to get through.

I was wheeled, bed and all, down to the operating room, which felt sort of like a carnival ride. It would have been fun—that is, if I was twelve, and not having a heart attack. As the staff shifted me onto a metal table and layered blankets around me, the cardiologist explained the procedure. For the angiogram, you're sedated, then they make an incision in your groin, in a major vein, and inject dye into you. Via a TV monitor, they can watch the dye flow into all the blood vessels in your heart, and any spot without dye indicates a blockage. If they did find a clogged area, the cardiologist went on, they'd do an angioplasty. That's where a tube is snaked up that same vein into your heart, and with a little roto-rooter balloon gizmo, the doctor cleans out your plaque. Instead of suturing your vein to seal it, they close it with this pop-rivet thingy. I could even watch the whole thing myself on the monitor—if the drugs didn't knock me out.

As it happened, I ended up falling into darkness and missing the whole thing. But as I opened my eyes, I looked up at the screen and saw a heart beating and blood flowing, and it hit me, *That's my heart and it's working fine.*

After surgery, the doctor told me the angiogram showed a small blockage, with two additional spots eighty percent blocked, so they'd ended up doing the angioplasty. While heart roto-rootering was no picnic, the real challenge came afterward. You've got to lie flat on your back for eight hours—and basically, *not move.* At all. Because any pressure on your incision can cause the rivet to pop out and you can bleed to death. Maybe people who are into serious meditation can lie still for hours, but since I'm not, I really struggled. After a couple of hours, I gave in and told the nurse how uncomfortable I was, and she gave me a sedative. Right away, I felt much more relaxed, and figured I was through the worst.

But…no. Being temporarily bedridden, I was given a plastic bottle for my "facilities." To use it, I would have to roll onto my side, keeping my legs in a perfectly straight line, and aim for the bottle. "But whatever you do," warned the nurse, "*don't sit up.*"

I don't mean to be indelicate, but trying to carefully roll and knowing the door was open to the busy hallway…well, I just couldn't relax enough to pee. As the hours passed and the aching grew, I thought of the stories I'd heard about women giving birth, when the pain gets so intense you give up all pretense of modesty to let Nature have her way with you. By mid-afternoon, I was in such agony I would do *anything* to urinate. In desperation, I asked the nurse if I could have a catheter. With that, like the old Alka-Seltzer ad says, "Oh, what a relief it is." Then I sort of floated through the remaining hours.

The following day, at discharge time, I was told not to drive for a few days, and not lift *anything*, not even a grocery bag. And only light activities. So I took a week off from work—the longest break I'd had in years. It wasn't until then that I realized how much I'd needed time to recharge, to *not* think about my job…and just *be.*

If there's one lesson I can pass on from this experience, it's this: if you're putting off a vacation, please don't wait until you have a heart attack to take one.

John's chest pain turned out to be a fairly minor heart "episode," as cardiologists will say. But it was the kind of wake-up call a lot of folks don't get. Like my dad.

The bigger mystery seemed to be, why had a healthy guy like John had a heart attack? He was only fifty-two! But it dawned on both of us that the stress of John's law enforcement career—and the irregular hours, especially night shifts—had taken a toll. Now in its twenty-ninth year, John's job had affected his health, perhaps permanently.

After my dad had his first heart attack, he told my mother, "It makes you lose your courage." I didn't want my husband to lose his— or any of the years ahead of him. Nor could I bear to see John ill and disabled, and track the years, as I'd done with my dad, by which care facility he'd lived in. If you can call it living. At my urging, we made plans for John to leave his job at the end of thirty years.

I'm happy to say he took his heart issues seriously. (Not like the patients who get a quadruple bypass, then on their way home from the hospital, light up a cigarette and head for McDonald's.) John followed up his hospital stay with cardio rehab, started fitness walking, and permanently crossed fast food off his what-to-eat list—which have given him top marks at his yearly check-ups.

With John's health problems behind us, and his subsequent retirement, we figured our routine would settle into a new normal. Yet more life-changing events, some welcome, some not, tumbled through our lives. I participated in a midlife miracle: the birth of our first grandchild. We lost my dad the following summer. John's sister was diagnosed with cancer. My younger daughter got married, and we gained another terrific son-in-law. John's daughter met The One and moved to the East Coast. My mom's whirlwind courtship with her first "boyfriend" since being widowed culminated with her remarriage, and a great new stepdad entered the picture.

As family dynamics shifted, John and I entered a new phase— embracing grandparenthood. As most grandpas/mas have before us, we learned this stage has all the joys of parenting, but none of the hard work. Our dimpled, sparky little granddaughter, who could have been her mom's twin at the same age, was the most delightful little person I'd ever met. Soon we were hitting the road a lot more, for visits or childcare.

That "feeling trapped" summer, along with our garden's inexplicable failure to thrive, also brought more road trips…sad ones. John's dad was diagnosed with inoperable cancer, and John began traveling to his folks' house regularly to help with caregiving.

So it wasn't only our noisy neighborhood that sparked our desire to "get out of Dodge," as John would say. Buffeted by the winds of change, with the occasional gust blowing us off course entirely, John and I longed to take charge of our destiny, in our own way. Longed for a new dream…to create something special and lasting. A whole new life.

7 ❧ Most Likely To...

My senior year of high school, I was voted "Most Likely to Succeed."

You have to see the irony. With no plans for the future, I married Terry at twenty, dropped out of college two years later, and by twenty-five, I was a stay-at-home mom with two little kids. Successful—in the conventional sense—I was not.

Some women approach homemaking as a career. I, however, wasn't one of them. While being home with my girls was important to me, it was also sort of a default decision. I just wandered into it—like an anti-goal. Always diffident, I had little experience with goals anyway, or making dreams happen.

In fact, for much of my life, I was the least goal-oriented person on the planet—what you politely call a late bloomer. I not only didn't find myself until well into adulthood, but I didn't even know enough to start looking.

But consider: what's the point of trying to "find" yourself? As the Zen people say, "wherever you go, there you are." In the same vein, how can you create goals, if you don't know what you want in the first place? But just before I hit thirty, I discovered a calling and formulated a real-life goal. I wanted to be a fitness instructor.

Several years before, soon after we'd left the Van H. farm, I stumbled across the perfect antidote for my trailer-trauma: aerobics. Popularized by the newly lean-and-mean Jane Fonda, aerobics quickly grew into *the* fitness zeitgeist—a lot like "Jazzercise," only guys could do it without feeling girly. It was like my first real passion, aside from my family. When you've dropped out of college, even to be a mom, it's easy to feel like an unmotivated slug. Especially when both your parents have a Ph.D.

But here was something I was good at, besides being Carrie's mommy. I was no longer an aimless college dropout, delivering newspapers three afternoons a week. Every Tuesday and Thursday, I'd race to the nearby middle school gym for my aerobics class, joining about fifty other like-minded souls for one solid hour of punishment.

Greg, the instructor, was a well-muscled animal, who fully espoused the "no pain, no gain" credo (before it became a no-no). This was pain. And you embraced it, pushing yourself until you got kind of sick to your stomach. But really, in a good way.

Then I got pregnant.

While the pregnancy was unplanned, it wasn't unwelcome. I continued the workouts, pushing myself even more, until my mild-mannered morning (and afternoon) sickness started to throw tantrums. The kind where I had to take myself out of class for a time-out in the girls' locker room, fighting the urge to puke. I generally viewed these episodes as minor setbacks, and tried to power my way through. But one day, after I'd spent a particularly long sojourn in the loo, I was forced to heed my body's message—one that even the most rabid fitness freak couldn't ignore: quit while you're ahead. My new passion was put on hold indefinitely.

A couple of years later, home with a toddler and kindergartener, I rediscovered aerobics. It was on TV now—anyone remember "The Twenty-Minute Workout?" The show had four young women with the most gorgeous figures ever known to mankind (womankind tried not to notice). This lissome quartet would gyrate seductively to the music, with the camera lovingly panning each curve. I, however, sought out a much more self-esteem-friendly exercise program.

I found it on Channel 2, Monday through Friday, led by a chirpy Canadian named Melody. Cute, but no supermodel like the Twenty-Minute babes, she incorporated dance moves into her workout, a lot like the ones I'd done in my college dance classes. Even better, I could easily do them without feeling like throwing up. For the next year or so, my thirty minutes with Melody became one of the highlights of my day.

Then we had to relocate for Terry's new job—sixty miles away, and outside Channel 2's broadcast area. Oh, noooo! I had to abandon Melody! Worse, we'd moved to a second-story apartment, with an extremely cranky neighbor below who would pound on the ceiling if you walked around on anything but your tiptoes. Even with TV populated by lots of new fitness queens like Kathy Smith or Denise Austin, in-house aerobics was no longer an option.

Happily, I found a nearby all-woman aerobics class that was more fun than Melody's show. As my confidence grew, I felt ready for something...well, *more*. Then one day, reading the want ads, I saw a job for a fitness instructor at the local YMCA. It was a sign from heaven: maybe I could do this! I, an introverted young mom, so shy I could hardly make phone calls, could teach aerobics myself!

Still, this dream seemed like such a long shot. I had no real training, no credentials—but I realized I *did* have two choices. I could remain a dissatisfied at-home mom, longing for a challenge, but paralyzed by doubt. Or I could actually make a move toward my first real, live goal and hustle down to the Y before the application deadline.

I picked Door #2—and never regretted it. The YMCA hired me *and* trained me. As an instructor, I discovered three wonderful things: I could overcome my shyness; I could get in front of a group of people and inspire them; and I could chat up my students and count backwards at the same time.

The real breakthrough, though, was figuring out that you *can* make dreams happen. But here's the deal—you've got to do more than wishing.

8 ❧ Y2K Not?

Does anyone remember Y2K? New Year's Day 2000, when every computer on the face of the earth was due to implode? (Meaning, the world as we know it would come to an end.)

I didn't pay much attention. At the time, my dad was having one medical crisis after another, in and out of the hospital and nursing home—and we knew he was never going to get better. I was also newly self-employed, working on my writing business seven days a week, while John, before his heart attack, was facing a heavier workload at the office.

"When the student is ready," goes the proverb, "the teacher appears." Browsing at Bellingham's Village Books one Sunday, we found *Sabbath: Restoring the Sacred Rhythm of Rest*, by Wayne Muller. For John and me, long on stress and short on sleep, the book's message—letting go of modern "busyness" for rest and renewal—hit home.

I started taking Sundays off: no writing, business phone calls, e-mail, or any computer work whatsoever. At first, I felt sort of lazy (my college professor parents had worked practically 24/7), but within weeks, I was shunning the computer as instinctively as if I'd fenced it with barbed wire. John and I swore off shopping or errands on Sundays (even dashing into 7-11 for a quart of milk was verboten), and set aside the evening for a date night. Observing the Sabbath felt so *right*—and soon we couldn't remember what it was like *not* to.

As it happened, post-Y2K, no computers exploded, and life went ticking on. But in taking a Sabbath, ours was forever changed—we could no longer reconcile the glaring incongruity between the peace within our household and the speeded-up world outside it.

Four whirlwind-of-change years passed. Coping with the tremblors shifting the family landscape—and after John had, for the first time, faced his own mortality—he and I needed something solid to hang on to more than ever. By our ten-year wedding anniversary, especially disheartened by Dad Browne's illness, we talked every day about wanting to move...and our drooping garden made it easier to contemplate. But that was all it was—talk.

Sometimes it takes a cataclysmic event to shake you off your foundations. For us, it was my sweet father-in-law dying only two months after his diagnosis. Suddenly, despite our sorrow, the idea we'd kicked around for years—to sell our house, get away from it all—took on a new urgency. The kind that told us, *if you don't do something now, you never will.* And John knew his country-bred dad would have loved what we had in mind: to buy some acreage "out in the county" as local people say, and dial down the pace of our lives to Crock-Pot slow.

But how to make such a life-altering change? How to get from here to there?

9 ❦ Rat Racing

For all my intentions to downshift my life, "slow" was not my default speed.

For most of my adult life, quick-quick, hurry-hurry was my standard M.O. Do more! Be more! Crank up those RPM's! And exercise was no exception. I tried jogging, but it gave me a massive stomachache. Plus my gimpy knee—a souvenir from six years of teaching aerobics—hurt with each step. So besides regular bike riding, I walked. Fast.

My revved-up pace was almost obligatory. I'm from a family of compulsive exercisers, who in their heyday thought nothing of swimming a couple of miles every day (one sister), or doing thrice-weekly self-directed biathlons: a thirty-five mile bike ride with a ten-mile run chaser (another sister and brother). Still, these same siblings razzed me about being a walking speed demon. "Trying out for the Olympics, Sue?" my brother would say. Of course, I had to walk alone, since no one I knew, friends or family, were game for my boot camp-y quick-step.

Strangers noticed it too. One day, walking in our neighborhood, I heard a girl call out from an upstairs window, "Go, Gadget, Go!" (For those of you who don't watch Nickelodeon, Inspector Gadget is a cartoon character who's always in such a rush his little animated legs rotate in a blur). On another walk, I sensed a group of young teens drifting behind me. I heard a giggle, and out of the corner of my eye I saw one of the kids imitating my arm-pumping, leg-stretching strides.

I had to laugh, but I admit, my gait was pretty uncomfortable. Nor did I really enjoy my walks—they were all about efficiency. Sure, I looked silly, but with kids/writing/a job, I didn't have time to slow down.

I'm sure I came by my speed-o-rama style naturally. My parents, both high-achieving academics, were the most driven, harried people I knew. With six kids, full-time teaching loads, and in thrall to their profession's "publish or perish" obligations, Mom and Dad's schedules were tripled-booked. Not surprisingly, they were late for everything. Late for their classes, late for our school drop-offs and pick-ups. Late getting dinner on the table, and even later getting to bed, writing textbooks and correcting term papers into the wee hours. Somehow, they fit in exercise too—my dad maintained a par golf game and my mother her cute figure. But with all this sleep-deprived rushing around, can you say, "stress?" My brother once clocked Dad—late for class, again—driving our '67 Ford station wagon ninety miles an hour down a two-lane country road.

I also inherited the late gene. To "get more done," I emulated my parents' night-owl habits, which naturally made for stressful, hurried mornings. After my divorce, as a single mom I worked more hours and had even less time to do more. Always behind schedule, I rushed to get the kids to school on time, to get to appointments, and to get to work, commensurately driving faster than I ought to.

And tailgating. Once day, racing to get my daughter to nursery school, I rear-ended another car. Luckily, we were both okay. But I didn't change my ways. I blamed hitting the car on my worn tires. Blamed the driver for slamming on his brakes for no apparent reason. And the lesson—a traffic ticket—didn't stick either. I had too much to do to drive slower. Live slower.

However, at thirty-eight, meeting John, I discovered a new and wonderful species: a person who didn't rush. After we got married, I also learned, to my astonishment, that he could get to work on time—or even early—without hurrying. When he took a walk, he strolled. And for any pastime, whether it was making pancakes or woodworking or creating garden beds, he had an easy, deliberate pace—that amazingly, proved you can accomplish just about anything without being a stress-case.

But hey. Wasn't I a working mom, pulling what they call the "second shift" and writing on my third? I was practically obligated to rush through life! By the time I hit forty, with my speeded-up walks—all for health, you understand—I sensed I was walking faster than was, um…healthy. I'd developed a nagging pain in my hips that wouldn't go away. Still, I wouldn't ease up. Living with that constant mantra in my head, *hurry, hurry, hurry!* I rushed through my walks, rushed through my days, rushed through my life.

And hardly noticed it. My life, that is.

John and I were still newlyweds when I started a new job—one that actually did make me "see" my life. But not in a good way.

The position—meant to be a stop-gap situation while I built my freelance writing career—was, in theory, creating marketing proposals for a consulting firm. But somehow, the marketing gig I thought I'd been offered morphed into a Girl Friday kind of thing. No, if truth be told, I discovered my real job was being the office gofer. Mostly for the office manager, Carol, who took the rushed, stressed-out mode of my parents' and kicked it up a notch.

A four-foot-eleven ball of energy, Carol spoke in a rapid-fire staccato, and ran the office with a brass-knuckled fist. Perhaps she had no choice—she was in charge of the company's financials for an owner who'd rather buy cars and fly his airplane than run his business. Carol was one of those people with an outsize sense of humor...but unfortunately, a temper to match. Out of the owner's earshot, her profanity would make your ears burn. (I'd been a Navy wife, but Carol could outdo any sailor's cursing I'd ever heard.) What really got her going was when the boss—whom we called The Big Kahuna—would pull stunts like buy a new Hummer when he could hardly make payroll.

Along with trying to corral the boss' spendthrifty ways, she was in the throes of menopause *and* caregiving for her elderly mother—which I admit could make even a saint fly off the handle. But used to ducking for cover from the Irish tempers in my own family, I found it hard going.

To give Carol credit, she never raged directly *at* me—I was simply the person she vented *to*. Still, the way she scurried around the firm's basement-level office suite like a hyperactive mouse, I could never quite escape her presence. You might think with all this rushing around going on, we were two of a kind, but I found myself eating *her* stress. I suppose my inward rush mode was hard enough to live with, without having Carol's constantly verbalized "everything is an emergency" to deal with too. Stuck with mindless but detail-rich chores like form-typing and spreadsheet-filling, I fell prey to Carol's moods and manic energy. And for an outdoor lover like me, being stuck in a basement cubicle with no windows nearby felt like being in jail.

On my lunch hour, I'd break out of the office like a schoolkid when the last bell rings, eager for light and fresh air. Setting an ever-speedier pace, I tried to walk off the frustration of doing clerical work when words and stories pulsed in my brain, bursting to get on paper. Once back in the office, I'd count the minutes until 5 p.m., count the weeks until the next national holiday, count the years until maybe, I could start freelance writing full-time.

10 ❦ "Feelin' Groovy"

You know you're a sad specimen when taking the morning off for medical reasons is a welcome reprieve, but that's how I felt the day I went in for a minor procedure.

"Should I go back to work?" I asked the doctor as she finished up, hoping she'd say no.

"Oh, sure," she said blithely. "But take it easy."

Problem: "taking it easy" and being at the office with Carol were mutually exclusive. (Have you ever noticed that after doctors have tinkered with your innards, they always say you can go back to work, even though you've got all the get-up and go of a slug on Valium?) Needless to say, I climbed into my car with the best of intentions. But I felt so weak and woozy I ended up heading home, and taking the rest of the day off. And not walking.

Back at work the next day, I couldn't wait for my lunch walk: the sunshine and scarlet sweet gum trees outside the office lured me outdoors. I set forth with my usual race-walk stride, and all of a sudden, my head began swimming. Even more disconcerting, my insides felt a bit…jiggly. Like the Simon & Garfunkel song says, I was moving too fast. I had to slow Waaay Down.

I didn't like it. My rush-mode wasn't just a habit, it was what I was all about. But as I took one careful step after another, it occurred to me that when your body takes charge of a situation, you don't have a whole lot to say about it.

The next day, my head didn't swim, but my insides still felt funny, and I couldn't walk much faster. The day after, I picked up the pace a little more, but somehow, the breakneck pace I'd set the last fifteen years didn't work for me anymore. I wasn't exactly stopping to smell the roses, but I was actually enjoying myself.

Discovering the joys of non-race walking was the start of my slowed-down life.

Not that I realized it at the time (we hadn't yet discovered the Sabbath book), although I did notice that my hips stopped aching. But the rest of my routine was still one big, hurried blur. Rush to work, rush home, rush to make dinner, rush to get some writing before falling into bed at two or three in the morning. Then rush to work a few hours later, for another unfulfilling day in my dim cubicle. One April day, I was surprised—make that gobsmacked—when the firm's owner, bless his dutiful heart, gave me a cute little violet in a blue ceramic planter for "Secretaries Day." (Before it turned into "Office Professionals Day," then more recently, "Administrative Professionals Day.")

Exclaiming over such a sweet gift, I thanked him profusely. And as soon as he left the room, I began crying.

Not a weepy kind of person, I'd *never* cried at a job before. But here I was, shedding tears over a pot of violets and couldn't stop. You may be thinking, how ungrateful—here the Big Kahuna was showing how much he appreciated my work! It wasn't so much that I minded secretarial work—I'd had lots of office jobs—but in my heart, I wasn't a secretary.

I ended up telling Carol I was sick and leaving work. Well, I was sick. Sick at heart. Sick that I had a college degree and publishers had considered my books but I was going nowhere with this job. Rushing toward home, frustrated about my career, even angry, I was practically nudging the back bumper of the car in front of me. Which had, obviously, a pokey, content-with-life driver at the wheel.

Hearing a siren, I glanced in my rearview mirror, and saw a police cruiser right behind me.

11 ❦ Busted

The cop was polite. I was mortified. I mean, here I was, a police sergeant's wife, going 40 in a 25 mph zone. He handed me a speeding ticket—my first ever. "Ma'am, I'm not going to cite you for tailgating," he said. "Although you were."

"Thank you," I said humbly, and drove home at granny-speed, thanking the Fates that I'd gotten only one citation. My careless speeding, in work-dollars, cost what I calculated to be nine hours of my life trapped in my basement cubicle.

That was the last time I tailgated any car. You know what else I learned? Driving the speed limit—or at least close to it—you can relax, since you're not constantly looking out for cops. Plus you can actually *watch the road.*

While getting a ticket didn't shift my entire mindset, I also discovered that speeding—not just with driving, but through life—is like wearing foggy spectacles. You have a perfect excuse for making wrong turns, or bumping into things. But when you slow down, the glasses come off. Your vision clears. You can "see" your life. And you're out of excuses when it comes to that infamous Dr. Phil question: "How's that workin' for ya?"

Years after my speeding ticket, when my secretarial job was only an unhappy memory, John and I faced the answer: our life in the city wasn't working for us at all. But like most people contemplating big life changes, we had to get uncomfortable enough with the status quo—our noisy, crowded neighborhood—to imagine something different. And man, were we uncomfortable.

As summer passed into autumn, John and I felt more and more like prisoners in our city-on-steroids…the city I once thought you'd be nuts to leave. Mourning John's dad, we yearned for a fresh start, a new life. But our real problem was…us.

John and I were prone to procrastination. We also resisted change like a two-year-old resists rules. My fitness career, however, had taught me something about goals. Unless you set a timetable and take an action, your castle in the air will never come down to earth. Here we were, hungry to pursue our dream, but we hadn't done anything about it.

Clearly, if we were serious about the slower, simpler life we craved, we'd have to take that first step. But did we have the guts, the audacity to try?

Even more crucial, did we have the cash?

12 ❧ Funny Money

Reinventing yourself takes the kind of courage I'd read about when I was a kid.

I'd cut my teeth on stories about Laura Ingalls teaching school at fifteen, Jo March going to New York to make her fortune, and Boston-bred "Mrs. Mike" venturing into the turn-of-the-century Canadian wilderness with her Mountie husband. For us, buying another, more expensive place to begin a new life—even if it was only a few miles outside of town—was surely in the realm of fairy tales.

For one thing—okay, the only thing—we couldn't afford it. (Obviously, if we could, we would have moved a long time ago!) We'd never been close to high rollers, and now that John was retired, our ready cash was limited. My own income as a writer and teacher was not exactly about "Show Me the Money."

And over the years, we'd allowed our "Street of Dreams" house to get a bit shabby—actually, it needed some seriously major improvements. The five-figure kind. To put our house on the market, these repairs would have to be done first. (Obviously, if we'd had the money, we would have fixed the place by now!) Talk about your Catch-22.

But a hopeful new development appeared: housing values in our region had taken a dramatic upswing. Our house might be worth far more than what we'd bought it for. Could that untapped equity give us the financial flexibility we needed? Was there actually a way to make our dream of living in the country come true?

Still, we wavered. Selling our house seemed so...well, scary. But you can only sit on the fence so long. You're gonna either fall off, or you've got to jump off while you've still got control.

One December morning, I decided to jump. I dug out the phone number of a Realtor a friend had mentioned, and said, "John, let's just do it."

It's not uncommon for folks to postpone making decisions, especially the ones that keep them awake nights. My take is, if more people realized what a relief it is to decide, they wouldn't put it off so long. For John and me, making that call lit a fire under us.

Since our dealings in real estate were limited—we'd separately bought and sold exactly one house apiece—we needed a Realtor with mojo. The kind who could make things happen. Jon was that kind of guy.

The mousy, rumpled-looking agent I'd hired years before had been anything but. In fact, if he were a comic-strip character, he'd have an "I really don't know what I'm doing" bubble above his head. Ask him any question, and he'd invariably say, "Um…" then, "I'm not sure."

Jon was the opposite. A sharp dresser with a crisp haircut, he had a "can-do" attitude that was contagious. If he didn't know something, he'd make it his business to find out.

Embarrassed at our house's scruffy look, on Jon's first visit, we pointed out all its problems before he could. When he proposed a selling price, the figure didn't exactly put the stars in our eyes, but it made our plan seem, for the first time, doable. "But," said Jon, "you've *got* to fix that siding."

The house siding was our Achilles' heel. Over time, it had morphed from slightly tacky to outright leaky. By now, the siding on the south wall, which took the brunt of the rain, was in its death throes, the saturated material swollen and buckling. Not just unsightly, but threatening the integrity of the structure. We knew something had to be done about it, whether we lived in the house or someone else did. We also knew that *not* repairing the siding and selling our house as a fixer-upper would mean dropping the price hugely—maybe by so much that we wouldn't be able to afford a new one. Which brings us to Nick, the home inspector.

We hired Nick—a referral from Jon—to lay out just what we'd have to do to get the house in top condition for selling. With the idea that you tell the bad news first, we took Nick outside to show him the siding and the rough repairs John had made. "I know, it looks pretty bad, but this is just temporary," John said. "For a permanent fix, what should I do?"

"Think like a raindrop," said Nick.

A Zen-like koan if ever we heard one. "You can figure that if there's any weak spots on a structure's outside," Nick went on, "water will find its way in. You could just replace the siding on that one wall yourself, but..."

"It would be better do the whole house," John finished, a little bleakly.

It was a job that John, despite his many talents, had neither the expertise nor the inclination for. And I wasn't exactly crazy about my husband—however intrepid he'd been in his law enforcement career—scaling walls and clambering on rooftops. We began calling siding contractors, and discovered re-siding the house would cost anywhere from "a few thousand" to twenty-five! Plus, we'd have to get the exterior painted—several more thousand!

It was like being stranded in Vegas with ten bucks to your name... and having to get lucky at the crap tables for your fare home.

John and I weren't gamblers. Nor were we big on living dangerously. Our idea of extreme sports was pruning trees and picking thorn-enveloped wild blackberries. To come up with the siding money, before the house sold, would take some mighty fancy footwork. Like walking a tightrope in stiletto heels.

Meanwhile, we could delay dealing with our teetering financial future with a winter pick-me-up: looking for a new place. Besides, what better way to brighten up a dreary Northwest February? So, to our "Wide World of Sports" pruning and berry-picking, we added extreme house-hunting.

13 ❦ Finding Neverland

Selling your place with nowhere to go may be an adventure for some—but not for us. John and I envisioned a seamless relocation process, from our present house to a county spread: sell, buy, close. Then pack up a U-Haul.

Since John was retired and I was a freelancer, we were essentially as free as the air. We could live wherever our fancy took us...and our fancy wanted to stay in the local area. For our new home's location, then, we had only two basic requirements: we wanted to move out of the city completely, and to a quiet location, with *space.* Happily, in the intervening years since my trailer experience, I'd transcended the frozen sewage trauma. Moving to a rural acreage, the bigger the better, was suddenly an immensely attractive prospect, septic tank and all.

I was ready. Country living, here I come!

At the outset, Jon the Realtor did what Realtors do and sent us online listings way out of our price range. After we told him firmly that we had to find a place for about the same monthly payment as our current mortgage, the dozens of properties trickled to a handful. Our "seamless" plan started unraveling as we realized that an existing home with a bit of acreage in our county was far more than we could afford.

Bowed but far from broken, we came up with a new plan. We'd buy raw land and build a house.

Since John and I were small town lovers at heart, we began nosing around several little communities outside Bellingham. Our county is mostly rural, with loads of open space, so we figured it would be easy to find land just outside one of these towns. There was land all right. We saw lots of pretty properties, most of them wetlands. Meaning you'd have to install a fancy septic system with mounds and pumps that would cost more than a mid-size car. Other lots were bordered by railroad tracks or had a gravel pit next door, with rock crushers pounding all day long. Or were downwind from a dairy farm. (Been there, done that…not doing it again.)

We ventured further afield, only to discover that raw land was rising in value as fast as homes in the city. You'd go on a property-search one Saturday afternoon, and two weeks later the price had gone up five grand. Given this new development, our procrastination, which John and I had honed to an art, would be our downfall. I pushed my writing and client work to the evening hours, and we shifted our property-hunting from more of a hobby to our Numero Uno priority.

Doggedly, we took to combing through the Sunday real estate ads, and made more country safaris several times a week. Still, we didn't find any properties that came close to "it." Then we saw one particularly promising online lead—five acres, far outside the city, and well within our budget. We jumped in the car and traveled thirty miles, to find that the parcel abutted a garbage dump masquerading as a cul-de-sac, the effect heightened by a gutted car lying upside down on the side of the road.

Disheartened, we made a U-turn, and ignored all the "For Sale" signs on the way home. How long could we keep doing this? Hours of driving around while my books went unwritten, our house fix-ups went unfixed, with nothing to show for it?

Then one Sunday, a newspaper ad leaped off the page—twenty acres, for an *amazing* price. We dropped the paper and got on the phone. Three days later, we met our new guru: Rick the Realtor.

To view this incredibly priced twenty acres, we got directions to meet Rick near the property and headed out of town. We passed immense berry and dairy farms, one of which was the never-to-be forgotten Van H. place. (Needless to say, the old mobile was gone. But the dingy, albeit newer single-wide replacement was almost as close to the cow pen as the trailer had been.)

As we drove further out, big farms gave way to smaller ones, with a few cows or horses. Then "farmettes," as a friend calls them, which are mainly a house with a bunch of ramshackle sheds, and a sprinkling of chickens, goats or sheep. (Or for the more creative, llamas.) Penetrating deeper into woodlands, we gradually gained altitude, and with each mile, the hills on either side of the road grew steeper. Well, if you wanted "space," apparently this was how far out you'd have to go to get it

Sighting Rick's pickup, we parked, then did the meet-and-greet. Rick reminded me of what must surely be the last of a vanishing breed: the gentleman cowboy. He specialized in rural properties, and knew *everyone*—who lived where in the area and how long. He even knew the people the local roads were named after. Rick also attuned us to the sad truth: most of the available land in our county was already taken, especially since the powers-that-be had gotten super strict about subdividing. But knowledge being power, we put ourselves into his hands and his massive diesel go-anywhere, do-anything Silverado, and trusted that he would lead us to our Nirvana.

14 Boonie Hunting

The three of us crowded into the front seat, and Rick took us for a short drive to a crude gravel road. As he downshifted, John and I craned our necks to gaze upward. This twenty acres were exactly where? The Silverado chugged up the steepest grade I'd ever experienced in a vehicle, and at the top we climbed out of the truck. And discovered that most of the acreage was perched on the side of a hill…no, more of a mountain, with just enough level ground to put in a house and a driveway. The view, I grant you, was magnificent. You felt like an eagle in his aerie.

But the usable land was a half-acre out of twenty. John and I exchanged a glance. "I don't think so, Rick," I said.

"There wouldn't be enough room for our garden," John added. Too right—I couldn't see doing a heck of a lot of landscaping on what had to be a sixty-degree slope. There was also a *minor* safety issue. In our earthquake-prone region, one halfway decent shimmy would no doubt send our house—and us—downslope.

However, John and I had learned a thing or three from Jon, our selling Realtor. When it comes to buying a place, your agent will always take you to the least desirable property first, to try to unload the tough sell. So now that we'd seen Rick's worst offering, things could only get better.

Rick took us back to our pickup, then we trailed the Silverado to a small development he'd heard about through his mysterious grapevine of farmers and logging buddies. It was a short plat of four five-acre lots, already in the county pipeline waiting for approval. The price was a bit higher than the hilltop aerie, but still affordable! And really, who needed twenty acres of mountain, when you could have five level ones? With a paved road, wells installed, and land already cleared, the place had a cozy, country-estate kind of vibe. John and I gazed around in dazzled silence. The homes wouldn't be all that far apart—you could envision a friendly little community growing here. "We really love it," I said.

"How soon will the parcels be on the market?" John asked.

Rick cleared his throat. "Uh…a few weeks."

His hesitation told me that "a few weeks" was really optimistic.

Since we didn't have the luxury of time, I asked, "Do you have anything else you can show us?"

"There *might* be one more place," Rick said slowly. Hardly a sure thing, then, but back we climbed into our respective pick-ups. John and I followed him on a narrow, two-lane road lined with Douglas firs and hemlocks, snugged up against the edge of the Cascade Foothills. I gazed at the forested hills looming above us, and said to John, "Honey, do we *really* want to live this far out?" On this overcast February afternoon, the area felt lonely and desolate. Definitely the outer edge of the boondocks.

Rick turned into a small horse and cattle ranch, and then onto a pot-holed, single-lane track behind it. John and I parked, and got back into the Silverado. Crawling along the rough, teeth-rattling road, Rick drove toward a ridge covered with jagged stumps and spindly, bare-leafed birch and alder trees.

This tract, Rick told us as he negotiated the potholes, was seven parcels of ten acres each. The catch was, only three were on the market—that is, kind of unofficially. The other four lots were tied up in a short plat.

By now, "short plat" set off warning bells. "Which parcels are actually for sale?" I asked. "Or, almost for sale?"

As we rounded a curve in the road, Rick pointed to a low-lying, scrubby area and said, "There's that one." The lot could have been in the dictionary under "stump ranch."

I barely glanced at the site—it was that ugly—and thought, *no way.* We meandered uphill, and came across another site that resembled a moonscape, with a huge crater in the middle. "Gravel mining," said Rick before we could ask. "But it's with the short plat."

Well, who'd buy a lot that was mostly hole anyway? Then we approached another brush-filled area overlooking the ridge. "That one's for sale," he said, pointing. "But I think someone's made an offer on it." Not terribly impressed, John and I peered at the lot as Rick drove past, until we reached the end of the track. "And here's the third parcel."

We scrambled out of the truck onto yet another brush-choked site. The entire development, including the parcel we were standing on, had been logged off six or seven years ago. Looking around, I decided that the only place you'll find more wood than in a forest is a clearcut.

The spare winter landscape exposed the rotting logs and tree detritus strewn everywhere. Sky, land, and vegetation seemed to blend into a depressing gray-brown. The clouds hung low, and on this unprotected ridge, a chill wind penetrated my jacket. In this bleak terrain, I didn't feel the coziness of the "estates" we'd just looked at. Okay, these clearcut parcels had five more acres than the ones we'd already viewed, but they were five miles deeper into the boonies. *And* $15,000 more. "I like the other place better," I finally said. "With the five-acre pieces."

"I'll ask around, find out when the short plat's supposed to go through," Rick promised. On our way back to town, John and I drove slowly past the five acre plots we'd set our hearts on. As soon as we got home, we worked the numbers on what we were already viewing as our "country estate." Buying the five acres was doable! The next Sunday, we drove back without Rick, to get a better feel for the area.

But the place was…different. On this calm, windless day, we could hear the hiss of traffic on the state highway a quarter of a mile away. Worse, frequent gunshots pierced the air. Problem: it wasn't hunting season. We knew the short plat wasn't far from a high-density neighborhood reputed to have a bit of a reputation. But as the gunfire continued, I got the feeling the area was more unsavory than I thought. More Wild West…and not a romantic, "Hi-Ho, Silver" kind of place, but more of a bars and brothel and the occasional shoot-out kind of place.

The constant gunshots freaked me out. "This is not good," I said. The quiet we sought would be hard to come by around here.

"I know what you mean," agreed John. He was a lot more sanguine about firearms, having worn one on his hip for several decades, but the magic had worn off for him too. We trailed home, discouraged. Given our lack of choices, John and I conferred again on the numbers, then he called Rick. "Can we look at that ten-acre parcel again?"

Tuesday dawned, that rare, Pacific Northwest winter day with a clear sky and gentle breeze. We met Rick at the entry to the potholed track, and again clambered into his rig. As we bounced our way up the ridge again, Rick confirmed that the parcel he'd shown us had indeed been legally recorded…that is, officially for sale.

As I climbed out of the truck at the road's end, I gazed at the mountain before me and caught my breath. Could this be the same place that had depressed me only days ago? The sky, such a pure blue it made your heart ache with the beauty of it, seemed clearer and brighter up here. In fact, everything did.

In the sunshine, red-twigged vine maples glowed, and vibrant green young firs, undetected in the murk of the previous visit, dotted the landscape. A hawk sailed high above us, coasting on the winter thermals rising up the hillsides. With the landscape no longer obscured by low clouds, I drank in the sight of the green-gray Foothills to the northeast, folding one upon the other like origami. This is it, I thought. Our Shangri-la. This is our dream.

That afternoon, I felt I was reliving my Minnesota childhood, tromping alongside Rick and John as we got a fresh sense of the place. With the dense brush and uneven terrain, it was tricky walking—in fact, you could barely step without your feet slipping on the limbs underfoot, or getting tangled in blackberry vines. But I felt a new, fierce possessiveness for this place. It's ours, my heart sang. It's got to be ours!

15 🍃 Our Own Little Tara

Who knew I could have such a lust for land?

Maybe it all goes back to my Irish forebears. That Irish longing for your own plot of earth is well-documented—at least in the movies. In *Gone with the Wind*, Scarlett O'Hara's dad tells her land is *everything*. "It's the only thing worth fightin' for," says Pa O'Hara. "Worth dyin' for." And Tom Cruise, playing an Irish tenant farmer circa 1890 in *Far and Away*, goes through hell and back to enter the Oklahoma Land Rush, all so he can grow potatoes on his own farm.

Irish land-hunger also runs in John's family—his McDonald ancestors raced alongside other potato-lovers in the Land Rush too.

To trace my newfound craving for acreage, I looked to my own Irish grandmas, Hazel Hennessy, my dad's mom, and Alice Monaghan, my mom's mother. Although both were granddaughters of 19th century Irish immigrants, neither was into real estate.

And two Irish peas in a pod they were not. Hazel Hennessy was genteel and retiring, and a dedicated member of the Women's Christian Temperance Union—which is like the League of Women Voters, only this group campaigned against liquor. So despite her Irish blood, "drink" was not in her universe. Hazel never had much money, but she was naturally "lace-curtain Irish" (as the old saying goes, folks who have fruit in the house even when no one is sick).

A larger-than-life beauty, Alice Monaghan was black-haired and green-eyed—like Scarlett O'Hara, come to think of it. And, like Scarlett, she enjoyed a tot of bourbon now and then. Mostly now. Alice's main claim to fame was being the "spit image," as the Irish would say, of Hedy Lamarr, the 1940s movie star. Although she was a wealthy matron who never missed morning Mass and *always* had fruit in the house, Alice was still terrified of being "shanty Irish."

Okay, I admit the Shanty versus Lace Curtain thing has nothing to do with fruit. It's more a state of mind. But surely, acquiring our own ten-acre Tara would forever keep me out of the Shanty Irish set.

16 ❦ Rolling the Dice

"One person's picture postcard is another person's normal," writes Barbara Kingsolver. And how I wanted this Foothills hideaway to be our normal!

"The view—it's like a Japanese painting," John said, back in our car. He may have spent thirty years as a police officer but he has an artist's soul. I took one look at his face and knew he'd fallen head over heels for this property just like I had. On the way home, as I took in the signposts we passed, it hit me—these were the roads I'd tooled along nearly thirty years ago, doing my newspaper motor route. If we moved out here, it would be like my life had come full circle.

But it would take money. Lots of it. Like I said, John and I weren't exactly rolling in rubles. Did we have the courage to make an offer on the place, and trust that we could get all our financial ducks in order? There would be no going back. Any miscalculation, and we could lose our small nest egg, and wreck our one and only chance to make our dream come true. Only John and I were about as fond of risk-taking as my refined grandma Hazel was of martinis.

Despite that big stumbling block, now that we'd found our dream lot, that piece of heaven with a view the gods would envy, we *had* to have it. Even if the price was way over what we'd budgeted. So, like Scarlett O'Hara had raised her fist to the sky, and vowed that she'd never go hungry again, John and I made our own pact. As we sat on the couch one March evening, financial papers strewn all over the coffee table, we gripped hands, and made a promise to each other.

As God is our witness, we would do whatever it took to buy "our" land.

I'm no stranger to unwise economic choices. I'd made plenty of them when I was heedless and young, like getting married before I could legally enter a bar. Then, when I should have been old enough to know better, I became a writer—a profession that can, and usually does, take years to make a living at.

In our early married life, John and I wouldn't have won any praise from Suze Orman either. We'd stick our bank statements into that pile of mail you keep but you never open. Instead of balancing our checkbook, we'd call the bank every once in a while to see how close we were to the overdraft danger zone. But after I left my awful job as Carol's gofer and became a full-time freelancer—which increased my job satisfaction by a power of ten, and decreased my pay by about the same amount—John and I had to shape up. That is, start a money diet.

Over time, we learned to cut financial fats (discretionary spending), reduce carbs (debt), and fuel our household with lean protein (cash, not credit). "Fiscally conservative" became our middle name. With all this discipline, we were primed for the simpler life we'd dreamed of...almost. First, John and I needed to embrace risk.

The first step was easy—meeting with Rick to tender an offer on the ten acres. The next move, however, would be a giant leap into the financial unknown. With almost no "walkin' and talkin'" money, we'd have to make a down payment on the property, *and* prep our place for selling.

Now, there was no getting around our biggest impediment. We'd have to deal with the house siding.

John began calling and e-mailing contractors. Then came days and weeks of waiting for bids. We soon discovered that with the regional building boom in full force, every contractor we'd talked to—siding, painting, even your basic handyman—was not only charging *two* arms and legs, but they were also in big demand, some with a waiting period into the fall.

The fall! It was only April! We had to get the job done *now*, if not yesterday.

John and I couldn't market our house until we fixed the siding; we couldn't fix the siding unless we were close to selling the house so we could pay the contractor out of the proceeds. And we had to sell soon—or our offer on the magical ten acres would expire before we could fund the down payment. This wasn't a Catch-22, it was more of a Catch-66. Add another "6" and we're talking *The Omen*.

Without the siding repair, we—and our dreams—were sunk.

17 ❦ Cosmic Cooperation

There really is something to that cliché about the power of positive thinking. That is, once you truly have faith that everything will fall into place—and I mean you are focused one hundred percent on making it work—the Universe shakes your hand, and becomes your new best friend.

It works even with issues as "tricksy" (as *Lord of the Rings'* Gollum would say) as finances. To be on the safe side, don't let the Universe hear you say, "I can't afford that." Because sure enough, cosmic energy will block the flow of money to you or whatever else you want. So, despite the financial chasm John and I were trying to jump, we put our eggs in the Trust basket. Believing with all our hearts we *could* afford the ten acres, we cobbled together a down payment. We also had to believe that the housing market was hot enough, and that we'd sell quickly enough, to keep our fiscal eggs intact. *And* that we could find someone, *anyone*, to do the siding. ASAP.

Remember Jon, our Realtor with mojo? He knew someone who knew someone who knew this contractor from Oregon. Who could do siding! And who had, miraculously, an opening in his schedule for our siding job. His bid was considerably more than we'd budgeted, but really, what was a couple of thou in the grand scheme of things? Besides, when the Universe manifests exactly what you need, you don't ask questions. You just hang on tight, because the ride is sure to be a bumpy one.

We wasted no time signing on Tom the Contractor's dotted line. The same day, we took out a short-term loan for *his* down payment. Tom's crew would arrive in three weeks. Meanwhile, John and I needed to hustle to give our house a beauty contest-worthy make-over.

Providentially, our income tax refund had just arrived. In the past, this annual windfall would provide a little cash for a personal splurge—for John, a couple of new Elizabeth Moon science fiction novels, and for me, a pound or two of gourmet chocolate. (I like to think expensive chocolate doesn't have the artery-clogging bad fats that the el cheapo brands do, but I could be wrong. If I am, please don't tell me.) But this year, we'd use every last penny of the refund for the new paint and fixtures we'd need.

Besides, who had time to sit around reading or eating bonbons? We had marathon cleaning, de-cluttering, and fixing to do!

18 🦋 In a Fix

John wasn't only a nature boy.

He was also a pioneer boy. He could, you know, do stuff. Build fires. Or fences. Clean a gun. Even skin a rabbit. Or as Harrison Ford, in the movie *Six Days, Seven Nights*, would put it, John had "skills"—most of which he'd learned from his dad. An engineer by nature and trade, Dad Browne could fix just about anything, with, as the saying goes, chewing gum and baling wire.

When I was little, my dad saved my life.

Well, maybe not my *life*, but close. One night, our family was having fish for dinner. I was chowing merrily away when all of a sudden I got a fishbone stuck in the roof of my mouth. Did it ever hurt! While Mom kept me calm, Dad fetched his handy-dandy needle-nose pliers and swiftly extracted the bone.

From that moment, I firmly believed that my dad could fix or do anything. (Well, not brain surgery of course, but close.) As a Kansas farm kid growing up during the Great Depression, Dad learned how to fix farm equipment like tractors and windmills on-site—in those days, no one could afford to outsource repairs. With an instinct for quickly seeing solutions, Dad went on to study mechanical engineering, and ended up at Boeing during the glory days of space exploration. As part of the Lunar Orbiter team in the late 1960s, he oversaw the power supply design for the lunar satellite, a precursor to the Apollo Moon Missions.

That was Dad's career highlight. But he was also big on DIY projects around the house. He always said, "Why pay someone for jobs you can do yourself?" Whether my dad wanted my brother Spike and me to learn home skills or just needed helpers, I don't know, but I got my first serious work lessons when he tackled landscaping our yard. I've read about the folks living in Ireland who have fields with more stones than soil. I think our place was a lot like the Old Sod, because Spike and I raked rocks for days.

For Dad's next project, building a shop, I learned to make concrete by hand. The Browne recipe: one shovel of Portland cement, two shovels of gravel and three shovels of sand. Then add water, mixing well until blended, using just enough so the concrete pours like thick pudding.

Dad also taught me how to level ground, hammer nails, saw boards, drill holes in concrete by hand, dig trenches, and lay concrete drain pipe. At the time, I would rather have watched "The Lone Ranger" on TV. As I grew up, though, I valued the skills I learned from Dad because they kept us connected. And now that he's gone, when I build things or tinker with repairs, I feel I'm keeping his memory alive.

Sure, Dad's fix-it lessons made it easier to prepare our house for sale. But the biggest thing I learned from him was that problems, even big ones, can be resolved. All it takes is breaking down the problem into components, then solving each smaller component one at a time.

It's like Dad always said. "You can't eat an elephant in one bite."

John may lack his father's engineering training, but he is happiest with a hammer or screwdriver in his hand. (Unlike my own dad, whose tool of choice was a 50s-era Smith-Corona typewriter.) For starters, John can assemble kit furniture when no one else in the family can make sense of the directions, though he'd rather build furniture from scratch. He can install faucets, repair leaky toilets, and operate huge power saws that I don't even know how to turn on. Constructing our backyard arbor, he made it as solid as a little cabin, with cool fold-up benches.

While he has loads of "skills," John doesn't necessarily have unlimited time with which to use them, despite being retired. As an active Mason, he's held myriad leadership positions in the fraternity—some requiring car trips to the far reaches of eastern Washington—and he's also employed part-time by his home lodge. He's definitely one of those retirees who can claim, "I don't know when I had time to work!"

But when it came to our fixer-upper, John would have to fit in not days, but weeks of repairs. Whether it was door locks, weather-stripping or worn toilet seats, you name it, it needed replacing.

Embracing our goal of selling the house so we could close on the property, I put my own freelance work, previously on hold, on an extended leave of absence. My days became consumed by to-do lists that grew like kudzu and meetings with bankers who kept losing our paperwork. Not to mention getting the house immaculate while coming up with new "Honey-do's" for John.

While I could clean with the best of them—hadn't I Formula 409'ed my way through a decrepit trailer?—getting supplies for those repairs meant taking on yet another time-munching chore. One I'd give anything to get out of.

19 🍂 Home Improvement

Y ou have to understand something. I'm not a normal woman. I *hate* to shop.

I'd rather scrub toilets than go to the mall any day. Even visiting the nearby giganto grocery/all-in-one store for life's essentials is my idea of a nightmare. But now that we'd embarked on our home spit, polish and shine, John and I were practically camping out at Home Depot.

As Ms. Outdoor-Girl, I was all about "decorating" our garden— not the inside of our house. In fact, I'd be the last woman to futz around with design elements, or make sure my furniture coordinated. We still had the "apartment white" wall color that had come with the house—along with plenty of scuffmarks. Before, I'd thought, who cares? If our place was reasonably clean and tidy, that was good enough for me. However, for selling, I had to not only paint the place, but get invested, emotionally and financially, in giving our interior all the love it had been missing.

That meant power-shopping. Trolling the big-box aisles, wishing I was anywhere but here, I had paint to pick out, as well as brushes, rollers, and drop cloths. Light fixtures and plumbing items. And serious dilemmas, like choosing new toilet seats. Basic? Oak-carved? Or cushioned? Whatever we bought, it had to look good.

After reading scads of articles on prepping your house for sale, I figured I had the process down to a science.

The goal, according to real estate experts, is to make your home look as impersonal as a hotel. While you're at it, they suggest that you emotionally detach from your place. You've got to see your house as a product to sell, or how else can you ever leave it? The good news is, detaching is actually not so hard, once you've made your home a dead ringer for a room at the Sheraton.

The bad news: letting go doesn't happen instantly. Since the previous summer, our garden's slump—as if it knew it was going to be abandoned—had helped me disconnect, but I had room for improvement. So I worked on viewing our home enhancements dispassionately...as things we were doing for somebody else.

The first step was to clear away all personal items from view—i.e., clutter. I have a theory about clutter. It's like a link to the universality of the human experience. Walk into anyone's house, and it's scarily like your own. Bills, coupons, and appointment notes have taken up permanent residence on the kitchen countertop. The bathroom medicine cabinet will be crammed with dozens of expired prescription containers (you'll see these in case you're among the twenty-nine percent of visitors who take a peek). And in the closets, besides an everyday wardrobe, there'll be outdated clothes and knickknacks that clearly haven't been touched for years. And probably never will be again. (You'll know this too because if you've looked in the bathroom cabinets, what's stopping you from peering into the closets?)

John and I had the usual house clutter…not all that overwhelming, but then clutter is totally in the eye of the beholder. I'd say on a scale of ten, one being completely clutter-free, and ten being one of those houses the fire department has to condemn, ours was maybe a two and a half. Our garage, however, was in a category all its own. While John beheld a place full of eminently usable items, or at least all full of potential, I found it Stephen King scary. It was packed to the rafters with boxes of fifteen-year old cancelled checks, mounds of crumbly dried flower arrangements, and decrepit athletic equipment, like my 70s-era Wilson tennis racquet that I hadn't laid a finger on since 1987.

Like house clutter, this kind of junk is probably universal too. After all, a garage is the repository for items no one has room for in the house, as well as things people intend to discard but have never gotten around to—only there's more dirt and dust on everything. Our garage, though, posed a bigger challenge. John is not only a dedicated *basic* saver (someone with a block about throwing things out generally), but a *woodworker* saver. So at house-selling time, in addition to the other refuse, our garage held more tools than a hardware store and enough lumber and wood scraps to feed a forest fire for a couple of weeks. (John will swear that every time he forces himself to throw away some stray widget or thingamabob, sure enough, he'll find a purpose for this lost-forever item a week, month, or year down the road.)

Without a doubt, for our upcoming move, I had a dual clutter-fighting challenge. To sell the house, I had to remove all our personal effects from view. Plus *useful* clutter had to be purged as well, since we had no idea what kind of storage space we'd have in our future house. So I turned myself into a ruthless assassin—*La Femme Nikita* of clutter. Everything not currently in use, every piece of paper, every trinket or tchotchke, every *whatever*, was game to be eliminated: shredded, tossed, or given to charity. Of course, if the item had sentimental value, my eradication process got totally messed up. (Like most Boomers, John and I had an endless amount of personal memorabilia from our kids and old family odds and ends we'd inherited.) Those meaningful items got packed up and trucked to our newly acquired storage unit.

But I had a sentimental attachment to one non-family, completely useless possession I couldn't seem to shake.

20 ❧ Left Behind

My old Macintosh Classic.

I'd bought it in 1992, nine months into my return to college. This skookum computer was a symbol of my new post-divorce life. And as a single mom, often hard up for cash, it was the one gift I'd given myself…no, *spoiled* myself with. I wasn't cool, I'd never been cool, but my Mac was. It contained the whole of my professional life—not only scads of term papers, but two or three finished novels, plus another half-finished opus about a hottie-but-unlucky-in-love college professor.

If there was one inanimate object in my life that I loved, it was my Mac. An elegant little machine, in seven years (mystical, huh?), it had never had a malfunction. And how could you resist its welcoming little smiley face when you booted up? But with the advent of e-mail—around 1999, when even non-techie people like me started using it—I'd forsaken my Mac and bought a practical PC. Since then, for six years, my sweet little Mac had been sitting on the top shelf of my office closet.

I'd chided John about hanging onto objects he wasn't using. It didn't seem fair, then, for me to keep dragging this computer around, even if it barely took up one square foot of shelf space. Time to bite the bullet.

I called Goodwill. Would they accept a perfectly serviceable computer, even if it was a veritable dinosaur of the technological world? To my surprise (and dismay), they said yes. So I deleted everything on the hard drive, but I didn't reformat it. I didn't want to saddle the Mac's new owner with trying to reload software onto an outdated, if not defunct, operating system. And if any future user wanted to recover my early novel manuscripts, they were welcome to them. No doubt, they'd get a good laugh.

I drove to the Goodwill drop-off spot, and a nice young man came right over. We unloaded a bunch of other items, then I brought out the Mac. Unlike today's computers, you could pick up this little beauty with one hand. I made one pathetic, last-ditch effort to avoid giving it away. "Are you *sure* you can take this?"

"Oh, yeah," he said, smiling. I reluctantly handed it over. Watching him walk away with my Mac, I felt like I was saying goodbye to a beloved friend…one I'd never see again. But despite my ache of regret, I averted my gaze. Nobody said starting your life over would be easy.

After breaking up with Mac, my determination grew to create a sale-ready place. But somewhere along the line, I couldn't be as blasé about leaving our home as I'd planned.

For me, the upstairs held bittersweet shadows of the past. My office had originally been my younger daughter's bedroom, and the bathroom across the hall was the one we'd allocated as hers. At sixteen, Meghann had gone through an interior decorating stage, painting green swirls around the bedroom, and splashes of fuchsia flowers on the shower walls. In both rooms, she'd attached colorful little angel stickers on the doors and light switches, one of them a small posy of flowers, with the words "Angels Welcome Here" curved over the top. Meghann also stenciled a quote on the back side of her bedroom window blinds: "One grateful thought raised to heaven is the most perfect prayer." (Source unknown.)

An impersonal "look" this was not. The designs would have to go.

It was wrenching, scraping her flowers off the shower tiles, and painting primer over the green swirls. I felt like I was erasing Meghann's presence in our house, abandoning my memories of her. The last day of work in her old bedroom, I decided to leave the prayer stencil alone...and not because Jon the Realtor said don't worry about it.

Swallowing the lump in my throat, I adjusted the blinds so the quote didn't show. And as I finished the bathroom primer job, I turned resolutely away from the room's blandness, with every trace of Meg's color, gone.

Because like a fish, I had to keep moving forward...or keel over.

21 🦋 Selling Out

With the last stroke of our paintbrushes, John and I had the house so fresh and new-looking we hardly recognized our own place. And now that we'd created the desired hotel atmosphere—all it lacked was mints on the bed pillows—we were nearly ready for the big leap: putting up a "For Sale" sign.

All we had left was the exterior—the siding crew would arrive the next day.

Well, finally we had something to drown out the skateboarding.

Having your house resided is like living in a war zone. I have the utmost respect for people who undertake major interior remodels—admittedly, it's much worse to have a war going on inside rather than outside. All the same, I was accustomed to my quiet little writer's life. Predictable and peaceful.

Had I, once upon a time, actually complained about the neighborhood racket? Now I learned what real noise was. The crashes and grinding and power tools roared around us, wielded by the crew, a rather motley trio. One of the siders reminded me of a pirate. He sported an earring and a bandana wrapped around his head like Johnny Depp playing Captain Jack, his tool belt subbing for Jack's festive sash. Completing the look was the tattoo of a topless, buxom lass on his bicep. They were a hard-working bunch, though—fueled,

I think, by can after can of Mountain Dew. As the crew tore off the old siding right outside my window, I'd be working at my desk, clenched in fear that they'd also cut into the electrical lines and fry my computer.

But John rather enjoyed having the crew around. He'd stay outside all day, watching the process, and learning about things like new flashing techniques (no, not that kind—*siding* flashing, which keeps water out), and chronicled the process on his digital camera. He sort of bonded with the crew too. On their last day, he brought each of them a giant cinnamon roll from Great Harvest bakery, which they polished off in about five seconds and washed down with another six-pack of MD.

Johnny Depp and his duo had no sooner packed up their tools when the house painters took over. With the windows papered over, our house felt like a cave—a sensation not unlike my secretarial jail sentence from days of yore. But I think remodeling is like the pain of childbirth. The result is so great you soon forget what had seemed, at the time, so unendurable. We got the house on the market the day after my 50th birthday.

But would it sell in time for us to close on our property?

When it comes to listing your home for sale, conventional wisdom holds that the timeframe is completely unpredictable. Your place could sell in weeks. Or months. Or, horrors, years.

Our house sold the first day.

I put it down to Jon's sales acumen (and the hot market back then didn't hurt). Still, selling so fast seemed like Fate at work—even if the buyer was a real estate agent who'd popped in the day before for a preview. A slim, Nordic blond in her twenties, Karen looked like a young Christie Brinkley. Her boyish husband reminded me of actor Ryan Phillippe. Together, the two of them were scary-gorgeous. And the celeb resemblance didn't end there—behind those pretty faces lay the shrewdness of Donald Trump.

After we accepted Karen's offer, we realized we probably could have set the price higher, especially since we'd somehow negotiated ourselves out of all our major appliances. But I wasn't going to fret about it. Nor was John. We had bigger worries—our race against time.

We had to close the house sale fast to get our hands on the equity, to pay ourselves back for the siding job. If we couldn't do it in time, we'd get hit with a big financial penalty. But what do you know? The Universe gave us another leg up, and John and I made our deadline, closing on the sale two days before the deadline.

The sale came with a twist. Our buyers weren't quite ready to move in, and we weren't quite ready to move out. So Karen, who knew the art of the deal, proposed one: John and I could rent back our former home for six weeks.

Fabulous! We wouldn't have to rush out and find a temporary place. But there was a catch. The hot housing market that had allowed us to sell so fast meant rentals had gone sky-high too. The price Karen proposed—the new "market value"—was nearly double our mortgage payment! Feeling we'd sort of been "trumped," John and I jumped at her offer anyway, giving ourselves time to finish cleaning our horror-movie garage, pack up, and move out. I told myself I was ready to leave. Once I'd gotten past impersonalizing Meghann's living spaces, letting go of the rest of the house was easy.

The garden was another story. Now that it was full-on springtime, the blueberry plants were setting fruit, the grapevines were leafing out around the arbor, and the blooming perennials were attracting scads of hummingbirds. Now that the backyard was no longer mine, I could hardly bear to enter it.

It wouldn't have been so bad if we'd been able to take our garden with us. Sounds bizarre, but I know lots of gardeners who'd done it when they moved. These professional-grade green-thumbers dug up pretty much all their plants, potted them or heeled them into a pile of soil in their new yard, and as soon as they got their beds ready, back in went their plants. Presto! Instant garden!

But Karen, savvy buyer that she was, stipulated that the landscaping would remain as is. Though we had a few divisions of peppermint and bee balm I'd potted the previous summer to take with us, there would be no digging up the stargazer lilies or the sprawling Cape fuchsia, a hummingbird favorite. Our nine blueberry bushes and the boysenberry that meant crisps brimming with fruit every July were hands-off too. John and I did take the liberty of pulling out a few tiny volunteers of honeysuckle, coral bells, and Japanese maple seedlings—the only plants that had thrived in the garden our last year—and potted them up. They'd be the first babies going into the ground at the new place.

So we had a house—and garden—to move out of. Now we needed one to move into.

22 🍂 Dream House

I like to follow the advice dear to motivational speakers everywhere: Dream Big. While we didn't have the time or money to go with a traditional stick-built home, the housing industry provided no end of options. Naturally, we wanted the best—which, as far as we could see, was one of those gorgeous cedar kit homes.

We visited the local dealer and paged through armfuls of catalogues. These log homes were stunning. Wouldn't the golden wood exterior fit beautifully with our woodland lot? You bet it would. And these homes seemed amazingly affordable. That is, until gentle pressure on the salesman got him to 'fess up to the real cost. When you factor in little things like digging a foundation and putting in plumbing, wiring and interior walls, you've added a cool $100,000.

Well, so long to cedar. I regretfully set down the catalogues, and met John's eyes. Reading his identical reaction, I said a brief "thank you" and we hi-tailed it outta there.

Still thinking big, we tweaked our vision and set our sights on another kind of dream place: a large pole building. Now you're talkin'! The construction method, different than traditional stick-built, meant you could create acres of interior square feet for far less cost. We'd seen plenty of these pole barn structures out in the country, imposing home/garage combos, big enough to house an army platoon.

We fantasized happily about a spacious great room, a couple of guest bedrooms for our kids and grandkids, even a library. Then we ran into the same roadblock as with the cedar homes: the price included only the exterior. The other mod cons (the modern conveniences mentioned above, along with luxuries like insulation and flooring) would still add six figures. Hoo-kay. So long, mondo-house dream.

Then we discovered modular homes. They were so cool—sturdily built, with intriguing floor plans and attractive features that you'd generally find only in custom stick-builts. But the only heating system available—wall-inset space heaters—was a deal-breaker. I'd lived in a house with an identical system for six years, and I've never been so cold in my life. All winter, my daughters, our little Springer spaniel and I would huddle around the few heaters, but all we got was dry hair, skin, and noses, and poor Lady got dandruff. I'd like to say that if the modulars had come with a nice gas furnace I'd be all over them, but the truth was, these homes were still about $50,000 out of our price range.

And somewhere along the cedar/pole barn/modular path we received yet another reality check.

As a city person, you never think about your utilities' infrastructure. You flip a switch, your lights come on. You turn on your faucet, and water flows out. You flush your toilet, the "stuff" disappears!

When you buy raw land for your new home, you discover the cost of your dwelling is only a starting point—you've got to put in all those utilities yourself. Let me rephrase. You've got to pay someone—a lot of someones, actually—to design and install those little things that automatically come with a city house, like waterlines and a water system, an on-site septic system, and electrical cabling. Not to mention carving a driveway to your home site.

Well. One thing about manifesting your dreams…be prepared to be flexible. And to "be with what is." When it dawned on John and me exactly how extensive this site development process really was, we saw that our "what is" was not a lot of bucks to spend on putting a roof over our heads. So we gave each other a pep talk and downsized our dream house fantasies.

We would have to go with the plain vanilla option. A manufactured home.

John and I headed to a dealer just outside of town, and met the head sales guy, a scruffy, unshaven older fellow wearing striped overalls, the kind train engineers used to wear. I've got nothing against overalls—hey, I could hardly wait to get a pair for working on our new place—but this guy's outfit looked like it hadn't been washed for a while. A really long while.

Right away, he directed us to his largest models. But armed with our new knowledge, John wasted no time asking, "How much does the site development cost?"

The salesman gazed into the distance. "Let's see." Long pause. "I'd say, about $20,000."

Ouch. Hardly peanuts. Peanuts that we wouldn't be able to put into the house itself. "You just roll the cost into your construction loan," he added. "It's no big deal." John and I took a breath, then looked through two or three models.

These manufactured homes were a bit of a comedown after the nifty modular ones, but this shopping experience had its own kind of charm. It reminded me of when I was a kid, and my dad would take my sibs and me to the county fair. Eating pink cotton candy or riding the Tilt-a-Whirl had nothing on exploring the camper-trailer exhibits. I'd pretend I could live in a tiny, sparkly-new place like these—like Laura Ingalls' Little House, or Sleeping Beauty's teensy cottage in the woods. Only cleaner.

Our sales guy escorted us into a bathroom of one model, and seemed inordinately proud that his toilets had a metal water intake pipe. "See, most manufactured homes have plastic." Since John and I remained unconvinced that this up-market toilet would make up for the rest of a pretty unremarkable house, we moved on.

Next stop was Birch River Homes, the top manufactured home dealer in the area. There, we met Dave the sales rep, a real smoothie. Clean-shaven, wearing a crisp, neat sports shirt with slacks, Dave could have been the soul brother of Jon the Realtor, another can-do guy.

Right away, John posed the $64,000 question. "How much for site development?"

Dave didn't hem, haw, or hesitate. "You should plan on at *least* $20,000. Maybe up to twenty-five."

I relaxed. Dave's range seemed more realistic, even to our green-horn ears. And it turns out the homes were manufactured in Oregon. John and I felt that was a big plus, that they were "Northwest grown." Kind of like the brand of chicken we bought at the grocery store.

Already impressed, John and I set off model-viewing, naturally starting at the high-end. We wandered through spacious triple-wides with fireplaces, wainscoting, and family rooms so big I could set up my own aerobics studio. But now that John and I had decided to dwell in the real world, we remembered there was the small matter of heating those sprawling 2500 square feet. "I, um…don't think we need all this room," I said to Dave.

He took us to a smaller double-wide model, with a layout we loved. And better yet, that we could afford. On our follow-up visits, John and I hunkered down with Dave in his office, creating our ultimate home with reckless abandon. And Dave made the extra features we yearned for seem so doable. The wrap around porch? We want it. Log siding? We need it. Metal roof, just the thing for the snowfalls you might get in the Foothills? We gotta have it.

We added these amenities to our purchase agreement, forked over the earnest money, and headed home to start packing. At last, our dream was actually happening!

23 ❧ The Asset

The "Asset," which I understand from *The Bourne Ultimatum*, is CIA-speak for a hired assassin. For our Foothills acreage—the one we shared with our bank, that is—we found an entirely different kind of asset. This hired gun proved to be our best discovery yet, not counting the property: Garrett, our site contractor.

If Rick the Realtor was our guru, Garrett was our Yoda. A veritable fount of knowledge and wisdom, Garrett knew meteorological systems, water systems, geography, and geology. Soft-spoken and easygoing, he had a centered kind of presence that told us he was The One.

Garrett, John, and I rendezvoused at the property, then surrounded by rich June greenery, the three of us did a walk-through of the house site. Garrett squinted at the steep hills ringing the area. "With all those hills, the runoff is going to continuously feed the aquifer down here. You'll never run out of water."

John and I exchanged a pleased glance. We were already cheered that the developers had recently upgraded the narrow, beat-up track into an up-to-code private gravel road and filled in the gravel mining crater on the nearby lot. With Garrett's assessment of our water supply, our choice of property was proving to be even more fortuitous than we'd thought!

Garrett was that rarest of construction species—an environmentalist site prep contractor. Instead of the usual scorched-earth approach—Rick could have put us in touch with any number of guys primed to clear and grade every last bare inch of our ten acres—Garrett asked us about our plans for our site. "Um, a house, and a vegetable garden?" I ventured.

"And room for some apple trees," John added.

Garrett rubbed his chin. "Let's clear a half-acre. That should be plenty of room." Then he went on about minimal clearing for minimal ecosystem disruption.

While I could totally respect that—clearly, he had greenie credibility second to none—I wouldn't have minded just a *little* bigger yard. But the two guys were already shaking hands on the deal.

At our next meeting, we discovered another advantage of hiring Garrett—he was a package deal. But no motley pirate-types for him. Garrett's crew consisted of wife Gwen, son Garrett Jr., and daughter Deborah, and as kin go, they were probably the most unusual—and I mean that in a good way—bunch I'd ever met. They were also living proof that the family who builds together, stays together.

Gwen wore her blond hair in two braids like a modern Brunhilde, and had just graduated from Huxley, the same environmental college I'd attended a dozen years before. As erudite as her husband, she was preparing to attend law school. Garrett Jr. was the muscle of the operation, a three-in-one handyman, driver and all-around assistant. Deborah, who was attending Huxley too, had colored her hair to reflect her environmental bent, an unadulterated kelly green. The extra plus of hiring a green contractor is that you can pretty much count on the crew not throwing their soda pop cans, cigarette butts, and burger wrappers all over your yard, as less environmentally minded types are prone to do.

Garrett also provided the voice of reality for site development costs. I guess the folks at both home dealers were either living in a dream world, or the finest liars I'd ever run across. Because the actual out-the-door site prep costs for clearing and grading, trenching, electrical, water and septic systems, and everything else was nowhere near $25,000.

It was closer to $40,000.

John and I read the sad writing on the wall, and returned to confer with Dave at Birch River. We pulled out our purchase agreement and started crossing off items. Gone was the wrap-around porch. The wood flooring. The log siding, the steel roofing. All those fabulous extras that screamed "dream house." But there was one amenity for our new place we wouldn't compromise on. We had earmarked part of our savings for a pole building/shop for John, with plans for partitioning a third of the floor space for his future office. Sure, we could have put that $20,000 into our vanilla house. But his office back in town, our tiny third bedroom, had been almost too cramped to work in. John, I felt, deserved to stretch out into his very own territory.

After years of dreaming about our peaceful country life, we had the acreage, the house, and the contractor. At long last, our new place in the Foothills was coming together...

Almost.

24 ❦ The Offer

You may be wondering where we were going to reside after our six weeks of renting were up, while our site was developed and home installed. So far, we had a piece of land with a well on it. And an order form sitting on Dave's desk. Not a shed or a shanty or a tent to stay in.

"Where are you going to live?" my mom asked one day, shortly after we'd sold our house.

"Oh, we'll find somewhere," I said confidently. Feeling like we were already country folks, we'd gotten a post office box in the village near our place, and planned to find a rental close by.

"You know, you and John could stay with us," Mom offered unexpectedly. "We've got lots of room."

Oh. My. I'd *never* expected this. "Uh, that's sweet," I said, not really taking her seriously. It was true that Mom and Burl, her new spouse of one year, did have room to spare, though most of the available space was filled with elegant art and the New Age-y knickknacks they bought on their travels. "But we couldn't impose."

I certainly couldn't. Even if it was for only a couple of months. Mom had mellowed hugely since her stressed-out parenting days, and we got along great. But I was fifty years old, for Pete's sake! Way, waaaay too old to crash at my mother's.

Since John and I were paying through the nose to rent back "our" house, we were prepared for a little inflation when we began searching for some county digs. What we found was two basic rental options—a really nice place that would hit your bank account upside the head, or a divey apartment or trailer next to the railroad tracks.

Faced with such limitations, it's also disconcerting when you're on a tight budget, and the people you know...well, aren't. Like your Generation-Y yuppie daughter and son-in-law. Already prosperous in their twenties, Carrie and Kevin had just bought a new speedboat. They'd hitch it behind their V-8 Toyota Tundra, for boating expeditions to one of the many lakes near their McMansion. My four-year old granddaughter Meghan, so demure and well-behaved, turned out to be a speed-demon boater. "Faster, Daddy, faster!" she'd yell, and her mom and dad would laugh, and crank up the throttle.

Little Meg may have loved risks, but like I told you, John and I couldn't afford to throw caution—or our money—overboard.

We followed up on rental ads, reworked our budget. No matter how we ran the numbers, though, we couldn't get away from one inescapable fact. We were sinking every penny we had—and some we didn't—into our new place. Any money we spent on a temporary home would be less money for the thousand and one things we'd need to start our new life. Especially less for our future garden, the biggest part of our dream.

I had one more of those face-reality, be-with-what-is kind of moments. One night, I counted the minutes until after 9 p.m.—Mom tended to be even more expansive and generous after her dinnertime glass of wine—then picked up the phone.

"Uh, Mom," I said when she answered. "Do you remember that offer you made a few weeks ago?"

PART II

"The oxen are slow, but the earth is patient."

—old Buddhist saying

25 ❦ Boomerang Boomers

You've heard of Boomerang Kids, or the Boomerang Generation, those twenty, even thirty-somethings moving back in with their parents. Given our...um, *maturity*, as John and I discussed Mom's offer, we faced at best, an unorthodox living arrangement. At worst, a huge mistake.

Bivouacking at Mom's, we told ourselves stoutly, could be a win-win situation. We'd get a place to live, obviously, and Mom and Burl, frequent travelers, would get two diligent house sitters who would care for the place like it was their own. Besides, why question Providence when It drops a goodie like this in your lap?

Airy and sun-drenched as an Italian villa, Mom's home featured a panoramic view of Puget Sound, an artfully landscaped yard with a container garden par excellence, and a kitchen with enough gadgets to stock a Crate & Barrel. John and I would have a cozy upstairs bedroom with a deluxe bathroom just across the hall. And after a decade of wandering in a TV-free wilderness, we'd have access to a dazzling, never-anticipated amenity—a monster-sized, surround-sound, high-definition entertainment center. Even the price was right. Our "rent" would be watering the flowerpots and setting out the trash.

Best of all, John and I got along famously not only with Mom, but with Burl too. What's not to like?

The truth was...I had mixed feelings about boomeranging. That is, besides the ignominy of a grown woman having to move in with her folks. John and I were still at the getting-acquainted stage with Burl, and I couldn't imagine a guy still in the honeymoon stage wanting his in-laws underfoot. And Mom? Well, she and I had never spent much time together. With four daughters, two sons, and an absorbing academic career, she was no helicopter parent. Since I'd eloped when I was barely out of my teens, she hadn't had much chance to hover over me anyway. And we'd never had much in common either—as an adult, I put my energies into parenting, and Mom put hers into teaching and writing. So in a way, I didn't know her all that well.

Naturally, it occurred to me that if I was better at earning the big bucks (John's retirement income was pretty well fixed), or even stayed at that soul-killing office job, I wouldn't be in this position. Besides, when it comes to visitors, I'd always believed "Fish and houseguests stink after three days." But the day our short-term lease expired, Mom and Burl would be in Britain, then off to China soon after. If John and I moved in, surely the four of us would be like those proverbial nocturnal ships—we'd hardly know the other two were around.

So I swallowed my pride, and with John as my accomplice, I launched a new trend: the Boomerang Boomer.

Since we'd done so much pre-packing, and Mom's was just a couple of miles away, I figured moving day would be a breeze. But I forgot to factor in the challenges of do-it-yourself moving after you're eligible for AARP membership. Moving Day turned into Moving Weekend—three days of last-minute packing, cleaning the place stem to stern, and trucking load after load of our worldly goods to the storage facility twenty-odd miles away. By the last leg, my fifty-something muscles ached like I'd done a 10K run, while John staggered around like he'd just crossed the finish line of the Ironman. We drove up the hill to the welcoming arms of Mom's empty house, stumbled inside gratefully, then slept halfway through the next day.

My friend Patty says, "When the gods want to punish you they answer your prayers." (From *Out of Africa*.) But our first, halcyon days at Mom's were hardly like doing time. In fact, as John and I leisurely unpacked, my misgivings about living at Mom's seemed silly. With Chez Parents to ourselves, and the crazy pace of the last six months over and done with, life was suddenly, blessedly easy.

John and I settled back into a new version of our old routine—

me, setting up shop in Mom's sunny dining room to write, and John parking his PC in our bedroom for his own work. After a productive day—without any moving-related phone calls or do-dahs to break my flow—I'd spend the summer evenings puttering on the deck, coddling Mom's potted petunias and Burl's herb-garden-in-a-barrel.

There's something very liberating about being home-less...um, home-free. Besides not having to pay a mortgage. Staying at Mom's, just the two of us, was like being on vacation. Her regular house-cleaner still came every week, so our domestic chores were minimal. My work was simplified too, now that my "office" consisted of a laptop and a box of files. Selling our house, I decided, had to be the best decision we'd ever made.

Still, in one corner of my heart I did miss our place—as if it was a child I'd sent off into the world, knowing they'd never be back. Since our old neighborhood was en route to most of my errands, I couldn't steer clear of it entirely. But I couldn't quite bring myself to go up our block and see our front yard, lush with summer growth. Instead, I'd take the street right behind it, and my gaze would go unerringly to the window of Meghann's old bedroom. When the blinds were down, which was most days, I'd see the prayer she'd stenciled on them, about gratitude being the perfect prayer.

I wondered if Karen, our financially savvy buyer, was too busy to remove the stencil. Or maybe she was as grateful for her life as I was for mine.

26 ❧ Déjà vu in the Woods

John and I had yet another consolation prize for selling our house—with our newly simplified life, we had several free afternoons a week. So we'd go out to the property, ostensibly to check on the pots we'd brought from our old garden.

Actually, we were revisiting our childhood.

Our first task, though, was practical—whacking out a small clearing by hand near the well, to set up a temporary plant orphanage. To make sure we wouldn't lose track of our pots among the heavy brush, we stashed them behind the biggest stump in sight, which our septic designer had aptly named "Big Stump." After giving each plant a slurp from the 2½ gallon water jugs we'd stored nearby, we would mosey around doing measurements for our house site. Then came the fun part for John and me: romping in the woods.

Today's superheroes, like Ironman, Batman, and Spiderman, are urban fantasies. I was a city boy myself, but when it came to *my* childhood heroes, I heard the call of the wild.

Country and wilderness stories fed my imagination: *The Lone Ranger, Rin Tin Tin,* and *Roy Rogers* on the radio and TV, and movies like *Davy Crockett* and *Treasure Island.* My mom would read *Robin Hood, Little Men* and *King Arthur for Boys* to my brother Spike and I, and I'd listen spellbound, secretly planning my own outdoor escapades.

Our yard had a mulberry hedge and when the berries were ripe, Spike and I would eat a few. But the rest we mashed and used as war paint for playing cowboys and Indians. When I got older, Spike and I got bolder. Inspired by Tarzan, we used a neighbor's block-and-tackle to rig up a zip line across a construction site. For other games, my friends and I would pull up bracken ferns, strip off the fronds, and use them as spears. I'd often go exploring solo, with a trusty spear in hand, pretending I was Robin Hood, an Indian brave or a Conquistador in search of gold. After a family visit to Fort Niagara, I got interested in the French and Indian War, especially the exploits of Rogers' Rangers. My pals and I would fill our pockets full of Douglas fir cones, and with me playing Rogers, I led the gang to take Fort Niagara from the French.

Since I tended to be on the bloodthirsty side, Fort Niagara especially appealed to me because it has a haunted well. Apparently around Rogers' time, two French officers fought a duel over a comely Indian maiden. The winner cut off the head of the loser, threw the head into the Niagara River, and dumped the body into a well inside the fort. The legend is that every so often, the headless ghost rises from the well, looking for his head.

While our property showed no signs of ghosts or other paranormal phenomena, the woods, untouched by dozers or excavators, felt magical to us. Unlike in fairy tales, it would take more than a magic wand to transform our wilderness into a home. With John clearly a natural at cutting trees and trailblazing, and both of us brought up with the Protestant work ethic, we tackled the job with gusto.

The Foothills weather didn't seem much different than in town— a little warmer, maybe—but we'd heard that winters could be a bit colder. And here we were with ten acres of trees! Given this virtually unlimited supply of firewood, John and I figured heating our new home with a woodstove was a total no-brainer. "Why pay the power company," John pointed out sensibly, "when you can heat your house for free?"

To ensure those cozy winters to come, we began collecting old logging slash that hadn't yet started to decompose, and stashed it in the brush. With his handsaw, John also cut down alder saplings and "suckers" sprouting off the plentiful red birch stumps, then we'd drag the twenty-footers to our firewood pile. You might wonder how a longtime tree-hugger like me, who'd embraced my environmental studies in college, could take on tree-destruction so easily. But when Garrett cleared the home site for development, these trees would get chewed up by his bulldozer anyway. Wood collecting and brush-clearing grew on me—which was fortunate, since there was so much of it to do. What surprised me was that it didn't feel like work. I was rediscovering what it was to *play*.

I'm not talking about the adult version of board games or sports, activities that take strategizing and at least some zeal for competition. But play as the childlike joy in simply being outside. It's the ultimate in slowing down, when you're completely in the flow, and time seems to stand still. You only realize it's time to quit when the sun dips behind the trees.

For me, this wilderness-taming business was every bit as fun as building forts had been, back in my childhood. The Foothills brush, though, was nothing like the civilized woods in Woodland Hills. You'd enter the thicket, dense with the heavy summer growth of bracken fern, fireweed, or thimbleberry towering over you, and more vegetation of every sort—trees, shrubs, and vines—would swallow you up, like you'd just donned Harry Potter's Cloak of Invisibility. And clearing could happen only by inches: take a step, bend to yank wood debris out of the way, and while you're down there, clip the six-foot tall weeds at the ground and toss them out of the way. Then straighten up to hack through ever-present blackberry canes.

You understand, these ubiquitous species weren't the genteel sort of cane berries like our late, lamented boysenberry back in town. These berries had canes as thick as a tree sapling, with thorns that could rip the flesh from your bones. Even a small scratch was not only painful, but would itch like the Dickens, as my dad would say.

Despite the dangers of blackberry wrangling, our carefree days in the country assuaged my grief for the garden I'd loved and left. Pleasantly tired from bushwhacking, John and I would head home at sunset for our free run of Mom's kitchen, and after dinner, we'd curl up on the couch in front of the giant TV for movies-on-demand.

The easy August weeks passed in a blink. Then Mom and Burl returned—and life changed abruptly.

27 ❦ Born to Run

People have remarked that I resemble my mother more than a little. But personality-wise, I'm definitely my father's daughter.

Dad was the introvert's introvert. When I was a kid back in Minnesota, he had a room of his own deep in the bowels of our split-level. Filled with bookshelves, a desk for the Smith-Corona, a tatty easy chair, and an antique leather-covered divan that belonged to his grandmother, Dad's windowless study was more like a cave. It was strewn with newspapers, stacked on the floor, on the desk and divan, and piles of them surrounded his reading chair like a moat. As a political scholar, I suppose he liked having all his research materials close at hand, even if they created a terrible fire hazard.

Looking back, though, maybe the papers were a way to keep intruders away. Not that you could blame a guy with five little kids for wanting a few minutes to himself...even a devoted father like mine, who was always game for horsey-back rides and bedtime stories. Although Dad never denied us access, we didn't exactly feel he'd issued an open invitation to stop in any old time either. We instinctively knew Dad liked his solitude.

When it comes to my own childhood fantasies, Dad's study must have inspired me, because I often dreamed of having a secret room all to myself. One that I didn't have to share with my sister, and better yet, that no one knew about besides me. (My secret place would be accessed by a hidden panel in my bedroom closet. But since my sister never paid much attention to the closet except to throw her toys and clothes into it willy-nilly, this fantasy was actually fairly plausible.) When I grew up to be a writer, a profession that demands oodles of solitary time, I'd found a career that suited me perfectly.

Okay, I'm not a complete hermit—like most folks, I keep up with a large circle of friends and family. When John is out of town, after a solitary day or two, I start talking to myself. Too, I love teaching, especially connecting with my students. But like my late father, after two or three hours surrounded by people, I'm looking to sneak off to a quiet corner with a thick newspaper.

With no quiet study-spot to call my own at Mom's, the day she and Burl flew in from Europe I had to relocate my office. No more laptop and manuscripts all over the garden-view dining table. As I set up my new worksite—a TV tray against the wall in our bedroom—I figured I was all set for home sharing. Plus, after eleven years with John, I'd learned to adopt his all-around philosophy of "Don't sweat the small stuff—and it's all small stuff."

How wrong could a Boomeranger be?

28 ❦ Period of Adjustment

When I was twelve, the most romantic cinematic experience of my entire life was seeing Jane Fonda and Jim Hutton in *Period of Adjustment*, playing shy young newlyweds getting used to married life. Like Jane and Jim, with our hosts back in residence, John and I had some adjusting to do.

Mom and Burl had hardly walked in the door before certain quirks and rhythms emerged. Right away, we caught on that Mom liked to keep her ivory carpeting and white tiled floor immaculate—and woe betide the blade of grass or fir needle that was tracked inside…or the person doing the tracking. I'd given up my late-late nights years before, but Mom was still an incorrigible night owl, and she and Burl often kept the Godzilla TV rumbling long past midnight. Burl was fond of a warm house, and as the late summer nights grew cool, he'd run the downstairs gas fireplace all evening. With the upstairs' mezzanine-type layout, the rising heat would turn our bedroom into a sauna, and my menopausal warm flashes into a nocturnal sweat-a-thon.

Funny enough, it was Burl, the stepdad I hardly knew, as loquacious and sociable as my dad was reserved, who greased the skids of our life at Mom's. Often, the more you get to know somebody, the less there is to like. Not with Burl. John and I discovered the guy who'd married my mother was not only a welcoming host, but a real sweetheart, with an outlook similar to ours in politics, religion, health, you name it. Burl had the generosity of spirit that didn't mind my dad's photos and memorabilia around the house, and he and John clicked like a Rubik's Cube.

At the same time, I discovered a new side to my mother…the way she supported Burl's passion for music, her grace under fire when dealing with challenging family members, a softness that being in love had brought. The four of us actually had fun together, often chatting over an evening glass of wine. Who wouldn't enjoy finding two new friends in your own parents?

So we learned to go with the flow. Shoes came off in the garage. The bedroom window stayed open all night. We learned to sleep through the TV din—albeit one foot apart (when I was "too sweaty for spoonin'" as my friend Lori says) to minimize my meno-BTU's. Besides, what were a few inconveniences? We'd be here only a couple more months. Or a "couple-three," as my dad used to say in North Dakota-ese.

It turns out we were laboring under a bit of an illusion—getting the construction permit alone took a full three months. When Garrett the Contractor finally phoned with the news, we flew downstairs to tell Mom and Burl. Surely it wouldn't take long to get the infrastructure installed…a bit of digging, then connect some wires and attach some pipes, right? And since we had a manufactured home, they'd just bring the two halves up from the factory and stick them together! Easy-peasy. We started counting the days until we'd move.

Even if we were short-time Boomerangers, there were some things my introverted, quiet-craving self couldn't get used to.

John and I have generally lived a fairly tranquil existence, you understand. We were accustomed to a slow start to the day, with a leisurely breakfast, each of us retreating behind our reading matter of choice. (Me, the *Seattle P-I*, and John, a good book.) Once we started our respective workdays, the only sound in the house would be the hum of our computers. And other than visits from our kids, our social activities were mostly off-site.

Mom and Burl lived on the other end of the spectrum. Their full schedules made the overall house atmosphere seem not just busy, but often frenetic. It was *nothing* like the low-stress life I craved. And the steady stream of people it took to keep Mom and Burl's household and well-being on track was, to me, mind-boggling.

There was a housecleaner, fish tank guy, lawn guy, and even a visiting masseuse. Mom had a research assistant/house major-domo, who also happened to be my darling youngest sister. So I had to fight the constant temptation to stop work for a chat. While Sis is the peaceable sort, her own posse included her pre-teen daughter at that tempestuous stage, and a high-strung miniature Dachshund.

Mom was writing a new book, one co-researched with a charming, vivacious woman a lot like Mom—she was even Irish. Adding to the buzz of activity, they would have frequent, animated brainstorming sessions in Mom's office next door. (Despite my need for quiet, though, some days they were having so much fun that sitting at my lonely TV tray, I was not only distracted but envious.) Mom and Burl also had regular visits from the scrapbook consultant, the computer consultant, and the heating-and-cooling expert who was convinced Mom's poorly designed boiler was going to blow up the house.

My personal nemesis—a small-stuff item that really got me sweating—was a fairly innocuous-looking household gadget: a talking thermometer. Actually, let's call it a "yelling" thermometer. At about 50-decibels, a sing-song automated female voice would bellow out the time (always wrong, p.m. instead of a.m., and vice versa) and the temperature. Also wrong. Then repeat this information at least three times.

I was in culture shock. Though I'd managed to recreate, sort of, a little oasis of calm by getting up early for a cup of tea, even that small ritual was often denied me. Because the thermometer would invariably go off—sort of like a bomb—right as I sat down to breakfast. The centered feeling I needed for writing (actually, for life) was eroding daily. And despite my steely determination to keep plunking away on my laptop, my productivity dropped faster than the Bullet Ride at the state fair. With solitude unavailable, and my work in shambles, I wanted to run away from home.

This longing to escape wasn't exactly new...I actually did run away from home once, at nine. Although I was the most biddable of children, the "good kid," and my mom's biggest helper, one day I was so fed up with chores and babysitting I did something only bad kids do. I talked my sister into skipping school with me, and we took off for the better part of the day. Though my rebellion was short-lived, my solitary nature stuck with me.

A few weeks into our stay, my Inner 'Tween was feeling all the constraints of living by other people's rules and schedules. And before long, my style—and I—was starting to feel more cramped than feet jammed into shoes three sizes too small. Simply flowing or not sweating or whatever wouldn't cut it.

I would need not just an attitude adjustment but a complete overhaul.

29 ❦ Family Ties

About this time, my daughter Meghann was moving from Seattle to her husband's hometown in Oregon. In early Boomerdom, I'd already been disabused of the notion that when your kids grow up and get married, your job as a mom is done. The fact is, you're still actively parenting, only now you're doing it long-distance.

With Meghann eight months pregnant with her first child, Carrie and I made the ten-hour round trip for a weekend move-in marathon at the new place. Four days later—though the baby wasn't due for another month—we got The Call from the expectant mommy, and our mother-daughter tag team, with granddaughter little Meg in tow, raced down I-5 again. We arrived at the hospital with only twenty minutes to spare, to help bring Meghann's baby Seamus into the world.

Some women see giving birth as a magical moment. When I'd had my babies, though, young and unthinking, I'd viewed delivering a child as something awful to get through. Now that I was fifty, it came to me that there are some transcendent moments, like witnessing the birth of your grandchildren, that you get only at midlife—when getting older feels more like a reward than a penance. As I cradled my newborn grandson in my arms, with little Meg drawing in a coloring book beside me, I decided my Boomer crow's feet and wonky back were a small price to pay for grandparenthood. Heck, if I got to help more grandbabies be born, I'd go through menopause all over again.

Soon after, I jumped back in the car for more traveling grandma gigs to Oregon and Seattle, to help with both the new baby and little Meg. While I got a break from Mom's hyper-lively household, at this stage of my life, caring for an infant and preschooler, I learned a new rhythm. You're fully occupied, fully engaged, but unlike when you're a mother with a to-do list a mile long, time ceases to matter. It's moments like these when you realize being solitary, always trying to escape from the hustle-and-bustle, feels kind of indulgent.

Immersed in the flow of life, I wished that the joy-filled October days with babies and little children and my own girls would never end. When it was time to leave, returning to Mom's for more Boomeranging didn't feel so daunting. I guess I needed to stay connected—to put down roots somewhere, even if it was at somebody else's house.

Of course, it helped that Mom and Burl were off to China.

Life, however, didn't necessarily settle down. One night, John's daughter Sasha called from the East Coast with thrilling news: she and The One were engaged! John got off the phone, his whole face one big smile. "They're planning the wedding for next spring!"

Grinning happily, I gave him a congratulatory hug. "Where's the wedding going to be?"

John's smile disappeared. "They're thinking of Italy."

Italy! My face fell. Sasha was John's only daughter, and the first of his two children to get married. No matter what it cost, he *had* to attend, even if I couldn't.

I wanted to keep my mouth shut, but really, I couldn't *not* say it. "Honey, how on earth can we pay for a European trip?" Our dream-house exchequer was already stretched to the limit.

John looked torn. You could tell he wanted to say, *I don't know.* But really, guys hate to admit that. So I took a breath, and thought, let it go. We'd cross that bank-busting bridge when we came to it.

Given that old saw about when the cat's away, the mice will play, I moved my laptop back to the dining table, and John and I got hooked again on the Godzilla TV. Despite the specter of the wedding travel expenses, I no longer felt quite so buffeted by outside events. That is, until one cold November night.

John and I were watching a movie when the phone rang. It was Carrie—my cool, self-possessed daughter, sobbing uncontrollably. "What is it?" I asked, panicked. "What's wrong?"

"The truck..." I couldn't make her out, she was crying so hard. "...In the lake."

"What? What did you say?"

"The truck...the truck rolled into the lake."

Dear God, dear God...Little Meg, only four, Carrie's husband... "Are you all right? Is everyone okay?"

In the half-heartbeat of silence, I felt a thousand terrors, lived a thousand deaths. "Yes," she said, still weeping. Fright still clutching me, I grabbed for John's hand as she told me what happened.

Carrie, Kevin, and little Meg had gone boating that Sunday afternoon. At dusk, she and Kevin parked their new Tundra on the landing, to haul the boat out of the water. As they loaded the boat onto its trailer, the truck's parking brake malfunctioned, and the boat *and* truck slid down the landing.

Into the lake.

Here was the miracle. Carrie and Kevin's usual drill was to secure Meg *in the truck* while they got the boat loaded. But that night, she'd fallen asleep on the boat. So instead, they'd let her sleep there, in the berth, instead of strapping her into the truck. If they hadn't, Meg would have been tight in her carseat when the truck went underwater.

Surely the angels were looking out for all of us that night. The horror of what had nearly been haunts me still.

30 ❧ "We Gather Together..."

After the close call with little Meg, life—and my loved ones—seemed infinitely more precious. And more fragile—that there's a mere razor-thin edge between everyday life and tragedy.

My dad told me that when I was an infant, I got my head stuck between the crib slats and the mattress, and when they just *happened* to check on me, I was turning blue. And these close encounters with the Grim Reaper are not uncommon. As a teen, my daughter Meghann didn't bother with seatbelts. Until the day she was riding in friend's little beater and a drunk slammed into the side of the car, totaling it—and for some reason, she just *happened* to have buckled up. Instead of being critically injured, or God help us, worse, she was only banged up, with a big welt across her chest from the seatbelt.

John's dad, as a kid on the farm, was once trampled by a cow, and he lost consciousness to the degree that he had an out-of-body experience. Then there's my brother Ty, the master of the close call. At six, racing to get outside, he ran not just *into* a glass storm door, but through it, leaving him with deep gashes at the wrist, elbow and temple. In high school, ever the risk-taker, he was racing downhill on his bike (in the days before bike helmets) and was hit by a car. He flew off the bike, smacking his head on the pavement, but was only knocked unconscious. A big skiing fan, a couple of years later Ty drove up to Mt. Baker in Dad's big Country Squire during a snowstorm. At a sharp curve, the heavy station wagon slid off the road, down the side of a cliff, only to be miraculously hung up on a ledge.

Incidents like these makes me think that life is simply a series of near misses—you, and everyone you know, are here on earth because of luck or angels. Or a combination of both.

So more grateful than ever for my supportive parents and the rent-free roof over our heads, I could welcome the return of our hosts, welcome the household regressing to hurly-burlydom. In fact, these warm and fuzzy feelings were a great warm-up for the holidays.

But I underestimated the effects of my FOO.

FOO, for the uninitiated, is not a play on "phooey." It stands for Family of Origin.

You know. What some people call your birth family, the people you grew up with. Also the people you generally spend your holidays with, and then afterward, wonder why.

Most people agree that once you grow up, you're free to create whatever holiday traditions you like, go to whomever's house or celebration you want to, come and go as you please. Or even stay home—though your FOO will have plenty to say about it. But when you're a Boomeranger, you no longer have that illusion of choice. If you have any sense of gratitude whatsoever, there's no getting out of spending the holidays with your parents.

So for John and me, staying put for Thanksgiving was a given— we would join the passel of siblings and houseguests for the long weekend. And this year, my FOO would actually be under one roof, sort of a rare occurrence. But not the good or interesting kind, like a lunar eclipse. More like the bad kind, like intense sunspot activity that blows out satellite and GPS systems.

Now, my own clan is no more quirky than the next one. (Growing up, I was convinced my family was really weird—I was at least twenty-five before I realized everyone's is kinda nutty.) As teens, though, my daughters hadn't yet made this discovery. One year, they created a customized Dysfunctional Family Advent Calendar for my FOO, and behind the cleverly decorated windows was some clipart illustrating each member's oddball behavior.

Whatever my girls think, I'm likewise convinced my tribe's holiday customs aren't all that different from everybody else's. Someone always drinks a wee bit too much. Also, every TV in the house is blasting with a cacophony of football, Nickelodeon cartoons and hip-hop videos. (The kind of shows you'd think people could forgo because a) they could watch this junk at their own house any old day, and b) they'd come all this way and could be chatting with the relatives they don't see very often. But apparently not.) Lastly, other family members will celebrate the holiday by saying whatever they think without editing for content. I'm the first to admit I can be as eccentric as the rest of them. Holidays with my family, however, present a unique challenge for me. Stuck in a house with twenty people, and not being a drinker so I've got nothing to take the edge off, I'm looking for not just a quiet corner, but an underground bunker.

Having accepted years ago that my family can be a little…overwhelming, I've always been big on holiday-themed self-help articles. You know, the ones that give you tips on making it though the craziness of mid-November to the second of January, the weeks of too much food, too much shopping, and too much family. All on too little sleep. This year, feeling I needed extra mental preparation, I reviewed my entire collection. Twice. Then I stumbled upon a fresh piece of advice. Since you can't change your family, to save your sanity you've got to do the changing.

How to do that? Easy, said the article, "embrace the mess." In the past, I'd changed myself by switching my holiday dinner locations. But this year, I was forced to change myself on-site. I had two choices of where I could go…insane, or with the flow.

I chose the flow.

Armed with the stress-reducing techniques I'd practiced for years, I was feeling quite smug that after three-plus months at Mom's, I had this flow mode down pat. And Thanksgiving Day was off to a great start. Mom's wine/cheese/crackers prelude was convivial, then Burl, my sister and I got the food on the table only an hour or two off schedule. The conversation went almost swimmingly, if you overlooked a certain relative's unfortunate tendency to remark on how much other people were eating. In fact, the dinner portion of Turkey Day was so pleasantly free of incident I figured the family had turned over not only a new leaf, but an entire tree.

By dessert time, though, things headed downhill faster than the Olympic bobsled event. Two of my fellow diners got into an argument—one that with a bit of grace, could have remained a mild difference of opinion, but in a blink turned into a firestorm.

[Cue lots of yelling while we're still at the dinner table.]

My pumpkin pie, one of my favorite desserts, turned to lead in my stomach. But as the quarrel petered out and the warring parties went off to their separate corners, I breathed a sign of relief. Now that we'd gotten the inevitable altercation out of the way, from here on out, Thanksgiving weekend would be smooth sailing.

Well, maybe…not. One of Mom's more volatile houseguests—who generally creates havoc wherever he goes—ministered the *coup de grace*. In the wee hours of the morning, the entire household was awakened by a huge crash. Our unpredictable guest, stepping outside for a smoke, had locked himself out. Having little impulse control, and instead of waiting until someone heard him banging on the door, he cut out the middleman by kicking the door in.

31 ❧ Back in the Saddle

You've probably heard of "Black Friday." It's the day after Thanksgiving that kick-starts the Christmas shopping season, when retail stores finally get out of the red and make some profit—are back in the black. At Mom's house, Black Friday is characterized by the Thanksgiving houseguests cooking themselves separate meals all day long and leaving their dishes for other folks to deal with. In this case, "black" refers to the mood of the ones facing a kitchen that looks like something blew up in it. And this particular Black Friday brought an all-new *lagniappe*—trying to find a repairman to fix the shattered doorframe.

Normally, the prospect of all this chaos would have me make like my dad and escape. But, I told myself, I could be strong. I could be steadfast. As the lifelong helper daughter, I could support Mom, "be with what is," and embrace the mess.

I actually believed this, for the rest of Friday and most of the next day (though my daughters would no doubt have added the busted-door episode to the newest edition of their advent calendar). Then my stiff upper lip started to sag. Tackling yet another sinkful of dirty dishes, I unloaded the dishwasher in silence, feeling powerless and immensely disrespected. Damn it, I own my own business! I fumed. I've written seven books! Why am I cleaning up everyone else's mess? I have Important Writing to do!

The back, I've heard, is not just the main support for the body. It's also where stress and stored-up emotion can hide out. Apparently my writer's spirit—one as easily bruised as the next writer's, and we are a very bruise-prone bunch—was developing a contusion the size of a holiday turkey. As my frustration built, I bent to lift a heavy bowl from the bottom of the dishwasher, and a spasm across my lower back hit me broadside. I gasped, and had to drop the bowl back on the rack. It was a pain like nothing I'd felt before, almost nauseating. It hurt so badly it took me several agonizing moments to even straighten up.

Back discomfort wasn't new to me—I'd dealt with sciatica for years. But instead of the usual dull, comes-and-goes ache, this stabbing pain stayed with me. For more than ten days, in fact, waking and sleeping. It hurt every time I moved. Forced to slow down, I did a lot of thinking about what caused my back to go out. Why here? Why now?

Well, I didn't have to be hit over the head. I hate to admit it, but the family baggage I was carrying, which I'd thought was a lone Samsonite travel case, was actually several ginormous steamer trunks. Turns out, those trunks are plenty heavy too.

You could even say I'd caused this pain myself. Playing my old childhood martyr role, instead of tracking down the dirty-dish perps to request that they step up to the plate—or in this case, up to the sink—and be responsible, for Pete's sake!

It also came to me that I hadn't embraced anything. Not the mess, the family, or anything else. Maybe some part of me figured that my plan to move out to the boonies, live the get-away-from-it-all life, meant you could avoid not only your family, but everything else that makes you uncomfortable. The truth is, you can't escape. Not from love *or* pain. And unless I wanted my back or some other body part to go out at stressful times, I would have to do a bit more of that "be with what is," acceptance I've been talking about. And not just during the holidays, but year-round.

Because when you get down to it, you can run from your FOO but you can't hide.

32 ❦ Breakthrough

No news is good news, says conventional wisdom. But when you're in the middle of a construction project, you want news. You want things to happen. As November came to a close, our property was a happenin' place. And John, with regular visits to document the site prep with his camera, was in on the buzz. Garrett was working every day, clearing the site and pouring the foundation, while our pole building guy had just delivered the lumber and started work. Even the earth moved…literally. One day, when John and Garrett were on a break, sitting on the stack of 2 x 4's, a minor earthquake almost shook them off the pile.

With all the excitement, my back pain and the memories of Thanksgiving were finally starting to fade. Then Dave, our sales rep at Birch River Homes, phoned with the headiest development of all. "Your house just rolled off the assembly line," he said, "and it's heading up I-5!"

I was so thrilled I almost dropped the phone. "That's great, that's so wonderful, I can't wait!" Surely we were only days away from moving out of Mom's!

"It'll be on the property by the end of the week," Dave confirmed, sounding as excited as I was. Maybe because he'd finally earn that commission he'd been waiting for, but still.

The following Saturday, a brisk, sunny morning early in December, the two halves of our shrink-wrapped home arrived. It was like ten Christmases rolled into one. Only our St. Nicholas wasn't a rotund elf with the white beard and red suit, but a radio-controlled little robot thingy. This undersized tractor, dwarfed by its load, crept up the long access road twice, pushing each half-house to the site. With John taking oodles of photos, the robot and crew nestled our new abode onto its concrete pad, then matched up the two pieces and married them together.

One eventful, challenging year—almost to the day—after we'd contacted Jon the Realtor, our dream, of living slower and simpler, was within our grasp.

Our life in the Foothills had officially begun.

33 ❧ Full House

Having a real, live house, on our own real, live acreage (even if we couldn't move into it yet) made it seem like our dream was finally coming true. Then again, like an optical illusion, the closer moving in seemed, the further away it actually was. At the same time, my boomerang fantasy, that Mom and Burl's travels and social whirl meant we'd hardly see each other, turned out to be exactly that—another illusion.

As our stay at Mom's lengthened, with all that togetherness, tension was inevitable.

It usually involved space...or the lack thereof. Children of the Great Depression, Mom and Burl were dedicated—dare I say, even compulsive—food shoppers, with a refrigerator and pantry more crowded than the beach at Waikiki. They had enough produce on hand to open a farmer's market, plus an eclectic array of condiments and delicacies like salad dressings, sauces, rubs, marinades and chutneys. (But no ketchup. Go figure.) The fridge in particular seemed to inhabit a curious shelf-space warp. You'd finish up, say, a sack of frozen peas, or head of lettuce, thinking, *Yesss—more room for my food!* as you freed up a few precious cubic inches. But before you could move in your own item, several new ones would mysteriously appear, crammed into the vacated spot.

Storage real estate was also at a premium. As a card-carrying neatnik, Mom relegated any household article not currently in use to the garage. Which, during our stay, overflowed with gardening tools, small appliances, extra furniture, giant bags of Costco fruit, an impressive suitcase collection, and an L.L. Bean catalogues' worth of outdoor wear. Mom and Burl had just bought a small vacation home, a transaction that included its entire contents. Now, they needed to find space for the deluge of dishes, linens, and enough kitschy doodads to fill a Dollar Store.

Storage needs for John and me were modest; we had a bunch of DVDs, baking supplies, and some tools. But given the demand for space, Mom cast a jaundiced eye on any box of ours contributing to the mountains of crud that formed a cave around her Crown Vic. Silent message: our clutter has no where else to go. Yours does.

Psychic space was even harder to come by. John and I, who thrived on solitude and plenty of it, had to share dual office space in our increasingly littered bedroom. Some days, in fact, I found it hard to believe I could live in such bedlam. Our room, strewn with sacks of groceries and boxes of files, office supplies, and personal effects crammed in between two computer stations, resembled Dad's study back from my childhood. Or worse—like it belonged to people with hoarding issues.

Boomerang telecommunication, though, really tested our mettle. Our well-connected hosts, home for the winter, were on the phone for hours a day to set up meetings, appointments, and social engagements. You could be diplomatic and say that phone calls or online time for John and me involved a delicate dance of scheduling and logistics. The truth was, we were more like teens always trying to sneak onto the family telephone, in the days before kids had their own cell phones from the time they uttered their first word.

Christmas at Mom's was surprisingly free of drama. Perhaps my family had used theirs all up after the Thanksgiving shenanigans. Or maybe I'd actually gotten better at embracing the mess. Anyway, with a smaller and more congenial group for Christmas dinner, there was actually a lot less of it. (If you don't count the heaps of gifts Mom and Burl had assembled, bless their generous hearts.) But John and I couldn't help sorely missing our own simple Yuletide traditions, with minimal presents, the air filled with the scent of cookies baking, and the muted sound of Old Englishy Christmas carols. Without a home of our own, Christmas didn't feel like Christmas.

And as the New Year arrived, I was starting to feel that life didn't feel like…life.

34 ❦ Stir-Crazy

Epiphany, then Martin Luther King Day came and went, and still our house was nowhere near ready. While I had writing and teaching to distract me from this odd, in-between life we were living, for John, time at Mom's hung heavily. So he spent the winter days out on the property. Staying warm and dry, sort of, in his brand-new Ruf Duck rain suit, John would tramp around in the winter drizzle, collecting more future firewood and salvaging any big landscaping-worthy rocks to stash at the edge of the clearing.

Naturally, there's only so much you can do on a building site when you don't have a dozer or backhoe of your own. So John would watch installations and framing and concrete pouring, meet subcontractors, and generally vacuum up knowledge—you know, doing that male-bonding thing—broadening his all-around skill set as Mr. Fix-it Junior. As he'd done with the site prep and home installation, he recorded the process with his digital camera, and even took pics of the house interior through the windows. Then, after a stop at our country post office box on the way home, John would arrive past dark, eyes bright with excitement, to share the day's mail and news. Once he'd downloaded the photos to his computer, we'd jam ourselves in front of it and view the house and site from every angle, over and over—like our small grandson who's always riveted by *Blues Clues* even though he's watched it 200 times before. But that's how hungry we were, to feel like we actually *did* have a home.

One January evening, John returned with not only a camera full of photos, but an exciting missive: a wedding invitation. Daughter Sasha, wasting no time on a long engagement, was tying the knot in May—and yippie, the wedding would not be in Italy, but California!

We could've jigged for joy. A European trip, even if John went solo, would've dealt a gigantic, if not fatal, blow to our house nest egg. And Santa Barbara, a beachfront town reputed to have beautiful scenery *and* soul, sounded like my kind of place. Still, John and I had little ready cash—make that none—for frills like travel. As dedicated homebodies, we weren't crazy about traveling anyway—short trips to the Seattle area and Oregon to visit family were pretty much it. Really, we were folks for whom the term "staycation" was invented.

But at this point, since we didn't have a home to leave, the prospect of travel fazed us far less than it would have. So like a couple of barnacles, John and I would scrape ourselves off our familiar rocks and routines. Come hell, high water, or any other calamity, natural or man-made, we'd make it to Sasha's nuptials.

We'd barely hung up the phone after our congratulatory call to the bride when our project went into the doldrums. Granted, winter is the least construction-friendly season of the year, but in the weeks that followed, long on gray and short on daylight, progress on our place advanced in fits and starts—mostly fits. I'm sure those of you more experienced builder types have already been rolling on the floor laughing (that's ROTLF in online-speak) at our naiveté—thinking we'd get our place done in a couple of months. We were a couple of greenhorns, all right, but I don't think anyone could have predicted exactly how thoroughly Murphy's Law ruled our building process. That is, if something could go wrong, it would. And did. Especially weather-wise—this particular winter was one of the rainiest on record. It was too wet for trenching. Too wet to set up concrete. Too wet to lay cable or water pipes.

Then, during the brief periods of non-rain, Catch-22's and mishaps ruled. We couldn't get the utilities' trench dug because our pole-building contractor and his concrete truck needed access to the site. Then he couldn't put up the metal siding because it had been damaged during delivery and needed to be reordered. The foundation guy couldn't install the cinderblocks because the cold, wet weather meant the mortar wouldn't set. And any time the weather would clear, his schedule would not. We couldn't get power to the house since the electrician had a death in the family and was taking a chunk of time off. When he finally got back to work, the pipe or cabling couldn't be laid until the county inspector had vetted the trench. Then after all the wiring was done, Garrett couldn't fill the trench until the inspector had returned to check the connections.

Despite his easygoing nature, John chafed ever more at the site delays, as well as our dependence upon Mom's goodwill. If the country regs had allowed it, he would have been perfectly happy to live in our house without water or power.

Because, you see, he was a veteran at what you might call Old Style Camping.

What's the difference between modern camping and the 1950's kind? Well, my friends, it's not RV's or cozy fifth-wheelers or even nifty REI backcountry equipment. It's the toilets.

Back then, a camping trip was really a working vacation. In the places my family visited in the Colorado Rockies, there were no real amenities. Especially outhouses. So Dad would create a row-pit latrine (behind some brush, for privacy), where you dig a long trench, then after you do your business, you cover your spot with dirt. The next user would then move down the row. (And if Dad made his calculations right, we'd get to the end of the row just as we were packing out.) Our family had a canvas tent with no floor, so we'd spread a tarp on the ground. Dad would make another trench around the tent, so if it rained, the water would drain into the trench instead of seep under the tent and into our sleeping bags. Dad would also improvise tables, benches, and water basins, and cleaned the fish so Mom could fry it up.

Naturally, it was fish he'd caught himself. Not one to loll in a lawn chair, Dad's idea of a good time wasn't just camping chores—he'd also indulge his artistic side. Dad was a fly-fisherman, so he'd always choose our campsites near a trout stream. Like all true fly-fishermen, he tied his own flies. He didn't arrive at the campsite with a tackle box full of them, though. He'd wait until he could observe the newly-hatched insects along the stream, then base his flies on what was in season. I always thought it was amazing how my father, who had really large hands, could create such beautiful tiny flies.

I never did do much fly-fishing, nor ever learned to tie flies. But watching my dad taught me something far better. Patience.

In our storage unit sat the used-only-once camping gear we'd bought the previous summer, now gathering dust. Ours was basic, though compared to John's childhood camp-kit, it seemed positively high-tech—a roomy, waterproof tent, propane camp stove, double air mattress with a battery operated air pump, a folding table and two comfy camp chairs. "We could rent a Port-a-Potty and live in the shop!" John exclaimed the day the builder finished it. "They're only fifteen dollars a month."

"Um, I think it might be a little too cold," I said uneasily. Although the prospect had a bizarre kind of appeal, I was what you call a cupcake camper. My youthful camping experiences, besides the one with my girlfriends, consisted of building tents with blankets and chairs in the living room of my childhood home. "And we don't have running water."

"Yet," he said hopefully. "Meanwhile, we could bring in some water—you know, in those five-gallon jugs."

Apparently for guys, showering can be put on a back burner. "It can't be much longer," I consoled him. "Can it?"

It could. More weeks dragged on with little progress...though the rain was having a field day. By the end of February, our area had received over a *foot* of precipitation.

And there we were, still with no place to call our own, as our lonely house in the Foothills sat in the sea of mud, unloved and unlived in.

35 ❦ Labor Pains

Back at the familial manse, as the long, wet winter slogged toward spring, John and I began keeping an even lower profile upstairs. All this time, Mom had been forbearance itself. But with the construction process dragging on, her good-natured questions about when our house would be ready grew more pointed. Our stay had surely turned into a movie script called "Guess Who's Coming to Dinner...And Staying Forever," and I could tell our worn-out welcome was reaching critical mass.

Given Mom's craving for order, I think the über-clutter of our bedroom—the detritus of two people living and working on top of each other—was finally taking her over the edge. (I was close myself.) Whenever she passed by the room (it would get incredibly stuffy unless we kept the door ajar), I think she coped by averting her eyes. One day, though, she peered inside and observed, "It's amazing you and John haven't killed each other by now."

The frustration John and I shared over our Slo-Mo project was actually sort of a bonding experience, at least enough to survive living in our shipwreck of a bedroom. But as the construction holdups continued to mount, one after another, accumulating like the slash we'd stockpiled for firewood, John and I had trouble keeping our spirits up. Garrett, our contractor, was juggling other drier home sites with soil you could actually work on, while the county and power company kept pushing back their timelines.

Our dream seemed mired in more than just mud. For the last year, we'd been proactive about making our new life happen. Captains of our little Foothills ship. Now, with Easter only weeks away and our lives still in limbo, we felt powerless, at the mercy of whatever subcontractor or inspector or weather system would show up—or not.

Although yogis and other spiritually attuned folks like Eckhart Tolle say that true happiness and contentment happens only when you live in the now, John and I were doing the opposite—dwelling almost exclusively on the future. Each evening, we'd visualize our new garden...how it would look, what food we'd grow, what we could freeze to eat year-round. Then, as we gazed at our house site photos, we'd refine plans for John's dream office inside the shop—how much lumber and sheetrock to order, what kind of floor to cover the concrete, and where to plumb for the half-bath we had in mind. The office, as John envisioned it, would have tons of shelf space, a TV, and even a microwave for snacks. It sounded so great I was a little afraid that once it was finished I'd never see him.

I personally had a barn on my wish list—the big, old-fashioned kind, made of wood and painted barn-red, naturally. But as the family number-cruncher, I knew a barn, like Santa and the Tooth Fairy, was in the realm of fantasy. So keeping our *doable* basics in mind, I'd pull out our house budget and we'd discuss all the purchases we'd need for our new life: appliances, tools, landscaping plants, and supplies. Our master shopping list, even *sans* barn, was starting to grow faster than "The Blob" of 50s horror movie fame. But of all the things we wanted, a woodstove, like cream, rose to the top.

One night, as we pored over the latest list, John said, "You know, with warmer weather just around the corner, we might as well wait until fall to buy the woodstove."

"Yeah, let's," I said, relieved. And not just for budgetary reasons—I actually felt sort of guilty about buying a woodstove. Let's face it, burning wood isn't exactly environmentally friendly. But maybe, I told myself, we could use the stove more as "backup" heat—kind of like when the doctor gives you codeine for post-surgical discomfort, plus a stash of Vicodin for "breakthrough" pain. Well, the woodstove could be our Vicodin.

While list-making didn't make the time go any faster, it did prevent us from committing house-delay hari-kari.

Just as I concluded our project was cursed, Mother Nature gave us a break.

With the spring equinox, the rain began to slack up, the temperature rose, and the soggy ground started to dry. At first, John and I were afraid to hope…would the weather actually stick? Could work once again commence on the property? But our elation grew as Garrett's pickup truck once again graced our driveway, and the home site started to come together. Power connected. Septic installed. Foundation blocks set in place. Garrett and Gwen put the finishing touches on the pumphouse, then began assembling the water system.

One sunny afternoon, I accompanied John out to the property for a look at the house. Since the entries weren't accessible, I picked my way through the mud and construction debris to the tall living room windows. John watched like a proud papa as I leaned in close, cupped my hands against the glass for blinders and gazed inside hungrily. It reminded me of long-ago springs when I'd take my little sister to the bakery after giving up sweets for Lent, and I'd salivate over the goodies behind the bakery case. Only now I craved a home, not an Easter bunny cookie. Even if I could only look, though, it was worth it. Beneath the skylight, the oak-fronted cabinetry in the kitchen gleamed in the sunshine, and the "great room" seemed vast after our cramped quarters at Mom's.

I turned to John, smiling so widely my face hurt. That day, instead of being a mirage that disappeared as you got closer, our new home had finally become a reality.

36 ❦ Vanilla House

A week later, with the drywall finished and the carpet laid, we got the A-okay to do a long-awaited tour of the interior. As John and I walked gingerly up the steep makeshift ramp at the kitchen door—Garrett hadn't yet built our entry steps—I felt anticipation like effervescence in my veins. I walked into the kitchen and stood beneath the skylight, joy filling me as expansively as light filled the room. The house seemed even brighter and more airy than the model we'd loved.

Then John and I slipped off our shoes and stepped onto the carpet—and my bubbles of delight popped. I peered down, and scuffed my toes around. "What's with this carpet?" It was scratchier than an ornery cat.

"It can't be the same kind that was in the model," John said, frowning.

We both knelt and ran our hands over the thin, Brillo Pad-like fabric. "It's worse than indoor/outdoor," I said, deflated, then rose to look with disgust at the expanse of super-cheap carpeting. "The cruddiest rentals I've ever lived in weren't this bad."

"I'm with you," John said, surprising me. "I'm a floor guy. I want a nice carpet to lie on. And a thicker one will help insulate the floor."

I could only imagine how much a new carpet would cost. "Maybe we could ask Dave about an upgrade," I ventured.

"It's worth a try," John said. "But this carpet is going."

"But our savings…"

"We'll make it work," John said firmly.

Who knew Mr. Rustic Camper would have such standards, I thought, feeling a little better. Determined to hang onto the magic, I put my carpet worries firmly aside. But with each step, I couldn't help taking in the glaring contrasts between our new place and Mom's. It wasn't just that the house was far smaller…it seemed so well, *plain*. With plastic everything. We had linoleum (a homely mix of grays and tans) instead of Mom's sleek tile flooring, flimsy closet doors (plastic) instead of her mirrored or solid wood ones, wobbly shower doors (plastic again) instead of Mom's glass ones. And half the rooms had no light fixtures, compared to Mom's lushly lit home.

Since I'd already kvetched about the carpet, I tried to hold in any more critical comments. John wasn't complaining, even if refinements like these didn't really matter to him anyway. Besides, it seemed self-ish, to put a damper on his excitement. So I told myself, *you'd better look at the bright side, because this is what we can afford.*

My glass-half-full approach had a setback as I glimpsed the floor molding—the factory-finished woodwork had more blemishes than a teenager living on Big Macs. But as soon as I quit dwelling on the flaws, I did start seeing our place with new eyes. Like the big pantry with its festive patterned-glass door. And the master bathroom with the foresty-green countertops, that seemed almost exotic compared to the beige-ish bathrooms I'd always had. While the house might be pretty basic, I could see it had a sort of Shaker-like simplicity. And it would be low-maintenance, much more than Mom's.

As I kept exploring, it also struck me that this house felt so *sturdy.* Nothing like the insubstantial feeling I remembered in the single-wide trailer back at Farmer Van H.'s, or every other mobile home I'd ever been in. (You'd suspect that if you stepped on the floor too hard, your foot would go right through it.) Even Mom's house would shudder and creak every time we got a windstorm. Amazingly, our place felt solid as a rock. Suddenly, this unassuming strength and dependability, so like John's, meant everything to me. Just like he feels like home to me, surely this house would.

By the end of our tour, we'd gotten plenty chilly—outside, it was in the mid-forties, and wasn't much warmer inside. Time to try out the forced-air electric furnace before we left. Within moments of flipping the switch, however, I realized the furnace was about the same quality as the carpet.

It simply blew a lot of hot air around—sort of like a Congress-man—without really warming the house. And it was obnoxiously loud (also like some politicians)—akin to simultaneously running a vacuum cleaner in every room. Besides, all that "wind" made the inside of the house as dry as the Dustbowl. And what was the point of moving to the boonies for peace and quiet if your own furnace drove you crazy?

I sighed, and turned off the switch. With this poor excuse for a furnace, we wouldn't be using a woodstove like Vicodin—that is, for breakthrough cold. It would have to be our primary heat source. "About the furnace," I ventured. "If we've got to replace the carpet, our savings will go really fast. And if we wait till fall to buy the woodstove…well—"

"Maybe we should buy the stove now," John said, reading my thoughts. "While we still have the money."

I felt warmer already. "The sooner the better, I think—who knows what else will come up."

Okay, I was a fair-weather environmentalist—it had taken only one cruddy little furnace to jettison my guilt and jump on the full-time woodstove bandwagon. While I could stick with my high-minded environmental ideals and freeze, why not adjust my expectations (after all, they'd been tweaked plenty already), embrace woodstove ownership, and be comfy all winter long?

I couldn't help hoping though, that Dave at Birch River Homes would make our bad carpet go away. As soon as we got back to Mom's, I called him about getting an upgrade.

"We can't do it," he said regretfully. Sales reps, I noticed, can express sympathy better than morticians. They're especially good at it when what they can't help you with will cost you a *lot*. "At this stage, it's too late to modify the purchase agreement."

"Could you buy back what's on the floor now?" I persisted. "Put it in one of your used homes?"

Hesitation. Oh dear, had I offended him? By saying *used* instead of *previously owned*? But then Dave admitted the carpet in our house was so cheap (my word, not his), that it would cost more to pull it up than it was worth. I thanked him anyway—after all, it wasn't his fault we'd assumed the carpeting in the model was the same kind that would be in the house we bought.

An expensive assumption. If we'd had the sense to ask, we could have ordered better carpet from the get-go, and rolled the cost into the home loan. Instead, John and I would have to come up with the cash for a good 1200 square feet of new floor covering. There was no time to waste either, since the house would soon be ready. So armed with a copy of *Consumer Reports*, and a bunch of store ads, the two of us hit the road. The big-time, power-shopping road.

37 🦋 Upgrades

If I'd known how much shopping was involved in reinventing our lives, I might never have started this whole adventure. Especially with last spring's house-selling purchases looking like peanuts compared to the big-ticket spree we planned. But I must say, shopping for items you get to keep is much less onerous than buying them for some stranger's benefit.

Hoping to support my local appliance retailers, I phoned them first. But the staff seemed not only unresponsive to my questions, but sort of unfriendly, so our first shop-stop was one of the big-box chains. We quickly chose a washer and dryer (Energy Star, which, I told myself, could make up a little—a very little—for using a woodstove…like trading carbon credits), then conveniently found a large selection of deep-freezers only one aisle away. Not wanting to make a second trip, we bought a freezer before we could remind ourselves it would be a long time before we had any home-grown fruits and veggies to stash in it.

Then we were off to the carpet shop to replace the cheap, cranky-cat floor covering. Figuring it couldn't hurt to ask, we inquired about wood flooring…only given the price, it actually *did* hurt to ask. Our fate would be wall-to-wall carpet, full of petrochemicals and glues and all kinds of noxious, outgassing materials that give your house about the same air quality as when you're standing next to a gasoline pump. Resigned, John and I figured a thick nap and bright shade would counteract the chilly, dark winters, so we chose something soft and blond—the Marilyn Monroe of carpets. It was nowhere near top-of-the-line; still, this unplanned-for cost made us blanch as we pulled out our checkbook for the down payment.

Saving best for last—a woodstove—we walked into the area's top heating and cooling dealer. We actually had plans for two stoves—we were going to buy a second-hand, much smaller one for John's garage office once he'd finished it. But for the living room stove, just as we had with our house search, we dreamed big. How about a granite-topped model? Or fabulous soapstone? Maybe Victorian-style, for that old-fashioned touch? You could even find stove exteriors in deep green or royal blue, with fancy metal fittings and trimmings that would make Martha Stewart drool like a teething baby. John and I browsed happily—I couldn't help caressing a smooth top here and there, thinking how this or that model would dress up our house. Then we started looking at price tags.

Bummer.

The little ones were $1800 and up. The bigger ones, the kind that would heat not only a room but an entire house—the kind we needed—ran $2500 to more than $3000. As much as I'd have loved one of these beauty-queen stoves, John didn't need to talk me out of it. Affordability-wise, there was Just. No. Way. As we did at the log home place, we quickly said our thank you's and vamoosed.

We were still committed, though, to buying brand-new for the house. My law-abiding guy didn't want to sneak an old woodstove under the state regulations' radar, while I wanted a stove with an excellent EPA rating, with the lowest emissions possible. But to paraphrase the old tune, how do you keep two shoppers down on the farm after they've seen gay Paree?

I clamped down on my uncharacteristic Martha S. cravings, and we moseyed on over to a more modest establishment. Right in front, as if it was waiting just for John and me, sat a sturdy black cast iron model. On sale, yet! And a price that sang to us: $999.

Sadly, the stove bore no resemblance to the fancy-schmancy ones. "It's kind of plain," I whispered to John. But to the salesman, I said, "That sale model's a great deal—any...uh, reason?" You don't want to say, *So, what's the catch? Is it an irregular or something?*

"It's on closeout," said the guy. "We're moving everything to our Stanwood store. If we sell this one now, that's a thousand pounds we don't have to ship."

"You can't beat the price with a stick," said John, all smiles. "We'd better get it before someone else does."

I nodded, firmly pushing away the lingering vision of gleaming soapstone. Buying this serviceable black stove, I felt like I was "settling," like the gal who marries Joe Average because he's reliable and he'll be good to her, instead of the handsome, reckless charmer she can't really count on but makes her heart go pitter-patter. But what a deal we'd gotten!

As the sales clerk made out the invoice, however, we discovered the stove price was only the beginning. There's pipe to buy. Installation parts. Since you can't park your woodstove right on your carpet, there's a fireproof floor pad of simulated tile. There's the labor to install the whole shebang. There's even a fee you pay to the state Department of Labor and Industries for the privilege of operating a woodstove. When all was said and done, there was a *big* chunk of change to add to that inviting $999.

Well. At least our firewood would be free.

38 Farewells

April arrived. And we were still at Mom's.

With all the rain, the snafus, and the construction delays, the brief stay we'd envisioned had stretched into its ninth month, like a stalled pregnancy. Any self-respecting obstetrician would have ordered an emergency Caesarean by now. Or at least induced labor.

For weeks, the drawn-out building process had been like having Braxton-Hicks—false labor pains that precede a birth. We'd be convinced the house and site—our baby—looked ready to be born, it would feel ready, and we'd had so many hopes that it would *be* ready...only to be disappointed. Like an expectant mother who is so tired of her unwieldy belly, swollen ankles, and heartburn that she'll do anything not to be pregnant, we felt we'd do *anything* not to live in that cramped and cluttered bedroom at Mom's.

As it happened, it was water—not breaking, but flowing—that meant our baby was finally on the way: Garrett had connected the plumbing! Within days, the water/heating/electrical systems had passed their tests, and the county inspector issued a permit of occupancy.

It was official...John and I would finally have a place to call our own! Suddenly, our little vanilla house seemed like a mansion. Despite our burning impatience to settle in, we figured we had no choice but to "camp" in it for half a week, until the new carpet was installed. But for us, even the prospect of a campout felt like a holiday at the Hilton.

Relieved, jubilant, we loaded up John's pickup and my small sedan.

Here we were, about to start our new life! But as our departure loomed, I was struck by an aching sense of loss.

Like I was leaving my family…for the first time.

I always felt I'd left home under a cloud. Back in 1975, finishing up my sophomore year at college, I was still living at home. Ever the helper, I'd stayed put to look after my adored baby sister, long after my two other sisters and all my friends had gotten out from under the parental roof. But right after my twentieth birthday, I was bursting with a long-postponed urge for independence. At the same time, my mother was struggling on all fronts—with the younger kids, her career, and my dad's new out-of-state job.

With our family's imminent move from the Midwest to the West Coast, I told myself I should stick around until it was time to go—if only to care for my sister, for whom I'd been a second mother. Instead, I'd cut and run. Found my own apartment. But in those few weeks on my own, I couldn't enjoy my newfound autonomy. I felt ashamed, like I'd deserted my mother—though I did my best not to think about it. (In fact, I suppressed my guilt so well that two months later I ended up eloping with my longtime boyfriend.)

Looking back through the years, I wonder if Mom had been too overwhelmed to lay a guilt trip on me, or even reproach me. Now, another reason occurred to me. Had she accepted my leaving as natural, when I hadn't? Whatever it was, she managed to line up a new university post, while selling, then packing up the house, all on her own.

Moss Hart, the playwright, once said of Julie Andrews, "She has that *terrible* British strength that makes you wonder how they ever lost India." My mother has that kind of grit—the kind that as a kid, I always took for granted.

When I was thirteen, and Mom was eight months pregnant, she took my six-year old brother and me to supper at Don's Drive-In (yes, it was exactly the kind of greasy spoon it sounds like). Little Brother, a non-stop talker, took a big bite of hot dog, and started choking. Suddenly, he couldn't talk. Couldn't breathe. As I froze in terror, not knowing what to do, my mother sprang into action.

Jumping to her feet, she grabbed my brother by the ankle with one hand, and despite her pregnant belly and petite frame, hoisted him into the air. As he dangled upside down, she gave him a vigorous shake, then another—and after a few awful moments, out popped the chunk of meat. Mom set down Little Brother, who apparently was none the worse for her '60s version of the Heimlich maneuver. He went on to finish his hot dog and Mom her hamburger. Life, as it always does, went on.

It wasn't until those long months at Mom's that I began to see what she was really made of. No matter what life has thrown at her, she's managed to roll with the punches—of jobs, family, illness, and grief...or kids leaving you in the lurch. Or kids that just plain won't *leave.*

That cloudy Palm Sunday, packing out of Mom's, I felt all the love and ambivalence and regret I hadn't allowed myself to feel that summer of '75. As I lingered with Mom and Burl in the entryway, I couldn't say "thank you" enough. Nor could John.

Mom had always been big on protracted goodbyes, and this evening was no exception. "Don't be strangers," chimed Mom and Burl, in the midst of the farewell hugs.

Feeling tearful, I joked, "I think I've got separation anxiety," but it was true. For the first time since I was a little kid, I would miss my mother. And with one last hug, I knew Mom's open door had meant far more than a place to stay. Maybe her hospitality wasn't as dramatic or heroic as her instinctive, maternal rescue back at Don's Drive-In. But then, as now, forty years later, she'd simply done what she needed to do to take care of her child.

She hadn't saved my *life.* But in letting us "boomerang," she'd saved my dream.

PART III

Adopt the pace of nature: her secret is patience.
— RALPH WALDO EMERSON

39 🦋 Foothills Wilderness

That night, when John and I trooped into our new house, we had a roof over our heads, running water, and our Congressman furnace. And not much else.

With our indoor "camp-out" (I was happily spared the Port-a-Potty/sleep-in-the-garage ordeal John had envisioned earlier), I admit this bivouac wouldn't be much of a wilderness experience. But as we toted our boxes up the kitchen door ramp in the dark, it felt a lot like crossing one of those primitive rope bridges in the *Indiana Jones* movies. With an inflatable mattress and two camp chairs as our only furnishings, and the shrieks of coyotes—imagine a pack of dogs on helium, laughing hysterically—audible through the closed windows, it seemed close enough to camping to make no difference.

The next morning, our first real day in the country, John and I awakened in high spirits, feeling like two kids at the kick-off of summer vacation. What fun, outdoorsy camp-adventures awaited us? But instead of being squished into a 20' by 20' campsite surrounded by perfect strangers (a typical camping scenario), John and I had ten acres to play in! The cleared half-acre around our house could be our blank canvas…like having a giant sheet of paper, with a 64-count box of Crayolas (my childhood dream, right up there with the secret room), to draw whatever we wanted.

Really, I thought as I walked into the kitchen, I don't know why I didn't get into camping before. I got my answer as soon as I dug a glass out of a box we'd brought from Mom's and turned on the tap.

You already know I have a bit of a germ thing going. But my inner

Suzy Homemaker wears green. I'm very anti-antibacterial soaps, and avoid Clorox or Lysol. When it comes to drinking water, however, I have my standards.

The water looked…well, *funny*. I held my filled glass up to the light, then wrinkled my nose in distaste. "Honey, look at this water," I said to John.

John peered at my glass. "What's wrong with it?"

"There's weird floaty things in it."

"Oh, that's nothing," John assured me. "Garrett said when you have a new well, there'll be a little sediment in the water for a while."

"How long is a *while*?" I asked suspiciously, then sniffed my glass.

"Uh, a few weeks?" John guessed. "Or maybe months."

Months of drinking water with orangey particulates in it? I don't think so. Even if it didn't smell like rotten eggs, like the other well water I'd had to drink, I dug my Pūr water pitcher out of another box, stuck in a new filter, and filled 'er up.

I'd hardly finished breakfast when I discovered those orange floaty things weren't only in my drinking glass. Already, there was a fuzzy orange film in the toilet bowls, though they'd just been cleaned a couple of days ago. Country living might be more rustic than I'd figured.

Once we got outside, I remembered another reason why camping hadn't particularly appealed to me: the bugs. Specifically, flies. The outside of our house was covered with them. Where had they come from? There were a few horses and a small herd of cattle in the area, but wouldn't the flies be much happier hanging around *them*? In pastures where there would be lots of nice fresh cow pies and equine road apples to climb around on? Then I realized the flies could have already visited such delights, and were now carrying all kinds of pathogens up to our place. *Ewww*. Though I barely cracked the door going in and out of the house, the flies buzzed inside like they had an open invitation.

But by the end of the afternoon—the usual time for my daily walk—it came to me that I had more problems than marginal water or germy insects.

40 ❦ Won't You Be My Neighbor?

Being firm believers in the old Swedish proverb, "The best place to find a helping hand is at the end of your own arm," John and I came to the Foothills with every intention of being self-sufficient. So I didn't mind that sightings of our nearest neighbors had been rare.

Not that they're actually *near*. There's a married couple living three-fourths of a mile down the road, their place completely hidden by a thick grove of firs, and the ranch down at the main road is one full mile away. As the crow flies, these folks are quite a bit closer, at about 200 yards and a half mile away respectively—albeit separated from our place by a steep, treacherous slope. But if you're not a crow, there's no way you're going to risk life, limb, and your creaky Boomer bones slogging down that hill, through brambles, brush, and downed logging slash. Not to mention a tangle of blackberry vines that'll trip you faster than a judo master.

Anyway, from the first time we put pen to purchase agreement, I'd known once we moved here that the only place to walk would be our mile-long private gravel road. But I'd never really thought about how *alone* I would be.

For a twosome who's fairly big on togetherness, John and I don't generally take walks together. My pace—despite my slowdown in recent years—is still what you might call vigorous, while John's is more moderate. Besides, I like the independence, and solo walks double as creative brainstorming time.

Freedom is all well and good, but venturing outside of our yard, on my own for the first time, I felt like I really *was* in the wilderness. Pros: It was quiet, and I had all the privacy I wanted and then some. Cons: Since all of the other properties in the seventy-three acre development were unsold or uninhabited, our gravel road was also *really* isolated—no passersby, no cars, no streetlights. Nothing.

I was all for country peace and open space and everything, but our remote location could mean danger. Might there be all kinds of wildlife—emphasis on wild—living on these deserted acres? Even in broad daylight, I could encounter any number of critters, like the deer I'd seen from the road and the coyotes we'd heard. All of which could pose some degree of hazard.

What about a hungry mountain lion? An aggressive doe protecting her young? (Sounds far-fetched, but I'd read about deer attacks.) A fierce she-bear, both hungry and protective? Besides potentially marauding coyotes, I could get attacked by a teeth-baring stray dog. (I'd already noticed most dogs in the country are big breeds—Labs or German shepherds or a mix of the two that invariably chase you.) Or a rabies-crazed raccoon!

There were also the perils a lone woman might face from two-legged critters—and I don't mean Sasquatch. But those, I categorically refused to think about. The crux of the matter was, if I really ran into trouble, my calls for help would be too far away to be heard. Or by the time anyone got to me, it might be too late.

So here I was, with all this Foothills beauty surrounding me, and I, generally no scaredy-cat, was being a weenie about going out on my own! I tracked John down, and babbled something about walking by myself. He let me run on for a bit, then said, "Would you like me to follow you?"

All the years we'd been married, I'd never played the girly card. *That's all right, I'll be fine*, I'd always said to his protective-guy offers. But today, I was all for it. "Oh, would you?"

As I strode down the road, John creeping behind me in his Ranger, it felt really indulgent to waste the gas—and totally wimpy to depend on him like that. But I felt a little bit like Dorothy entering the Land of Oz—in an all-new world, you can't always get by with the tried-and-true. Unlike Dorothy's time in Oz, my walk was without incident, save for the curious stares of the deer. The next day, after John trailed me a second time, and the deer paid absolutely no attention to me at all, I felt downright silly.

Well. This was my new life—and John wouldn't always be around to look after me. So, I vowed, I'd better develop a little fearlessness, or die trying. On Day Three, I told John I'd go alone, and took an umbrella even though there was nary a rain cloud in the sky. (Brandishing your bumbershoot will convince most growling dogs, at least, to keep their distance.) While the umbrella thing felt totally ridiculous, everybody knows what doesn't kill you—in this case, embarrassment—will make you stronger.

My walks might have been quiet and solitary, but our house was hoppin'. During our three-day camp-out, Garrett and his crowd were working in the yard, and we'd had a full day with Ray the woodstove installer in and out of the house, down in the crawl space and up on the roof. The next day, two guys from the flooring store took over the house, laying carpet with the speed and precision of a military maneuver.

After the carpet guys cleared out, John and I flopped onto our camp chairs for another sandwich dinner. Since we arrived, we'd hardly had a moment to ourselves. But in a funny kind of way, these three days had felt like a honeymoon. Only better. I smiled at John, thinking that over the long wait to get here, our marriage had not only survived, but thrived, despite the months of uncertainty, the extra work, and the enforced togetherness.

I think I'd come out of this a better person—a little less picky (if you didn't count my squeamishness about the orange water and flies), more flexible. John had grown even more patient, but then, he's always been a grin-and-bear-it, do-what-it-takes kind of guy.

With all that personal growth going on, we were a couple of walking self-help books, prepared for anything. Especially for tomorrow, our *real* Move-In Day.

41 🐛 It's Official

I have moving issues.

When it came to housing, my former husband lived the cliché, "the grass is always greener…" But not only on the other side of the fence. No matter where we lived, Terry was always itching to relocate: to another apartment, another house, another side of town, or another city entirely. And I, like the good little wife I was, would go along with it.

Was I simply emulating Ma Ingalls, Laura's mother in the "Little House" series, who'd stoically followed Pa and his wandering foot all over the Midwest? Or did I have an overcooked noodle where my backbone was supposed to be? Whatever it was, between my ex-spouse's thirst for new places and his job hopping (ten jobs in fourteen years of marriage), we moved seventeen times.

My daughter Carrie is also drawn to greener grass, with eleven moves in the twelve years she's been on her own. Compared to her sister, Meghann is an amateur—she can claim only six places. And except for two instances, I've helped both daughters move each time. Doing the math, once I throw in three post-divorce moves and John's and my first place, the numbers get kind of scary. From leaving home when I was twenty, by the time John and I crossed the threshold of our new Foothills house, I'd been involved in upwards of three dozen moves.

Of course, no one *likes* to move, but is it any wonder that I approach the process with all the enthusiasm of a Puritan facing a long day in the stocks? Yet there was another, more subtle twist to our country relocation. For John and me, this would be our last move. Our last house. If life went as we envisioned, the only way we'd leave our new place permanently would be feet first.

Moving angst or not, I'm the first to admit that moving *in* is much more fun than moving *out*. After our three days of camping, we were partly moved in anyway. And with heavy lifters John and George, the police officer friend we'd lined up to help us, I just knew the process would go smoothly.

All good reasons to forget my thirty-six-move burnout.

When you live in the city, you take things like sidewalks for granted. You get easy access to your door, plus it's easy to keep your shoes clean.

Our fourth day in the Foothills, I gazed out at our vegetation-free yard and the heavy rain that had begun before dawn. The empty canvas, that had seemed so full of potential a short time ago, was actually going to be a moving nightmare. Although Garrett had just finished the steps for each entrance into the house, for walkways, all we had was straw laid over the muddy ground. The terrain around the house, already compacted from excavating, was full of deep ruts. And now those ruts were full of water.

And through this muddy morass, two middle-aged guys and I would have to fetch an entire houseful of boxes and furniture from the U-Haul in our gravel driveway, then trudge through the moat surrounding our house to get it inside.

Maybe it wouldn't have been such a dismal prospect if we could've used the kitchen door—a mere hop, skip and jump to the driveway. But that entry, opening to a cramped mud room, had no space for maneuvering. Instead, John and George would have to trek around the corner to the sliding glass door in the living room. Compounding our logistical challenges, to spare our new blond carpet, I wouldn't let the guys actually enter the house. So it was up to me to push, pull, or heave whatever they hauled to the door all the way inside, then shove the object aside to make room for the next one.

As an extra precaution, I created pathways on the carpet with heavy-duty plastic garbage sacks. On this dark, rain-soaked day, the black plastic gave our place a funereal air, the slippery material adding yet another hazard.

It's a good thing both guys were used to being out in the weather. Although George was now a detective, and John's police days were behind him, they'd spent many a shift directing traffic, doing foot patrol, and making traffic stops no matter how hard it was raining. So without complaint, they put on rain jackets and set to it—wrapping each item from the truck in a blanket to keep it relatively dry, then slogging through the puddles around the corner of the house. Unfortunately, the coverings would often loosen and drag on the ground, so I had to safeguard the carpet from dirty wet blankets, as well as the guys' mud-caked boots.

Anyway, our system worked…okay. Until we came to my nemesis: the couch.

When you choose a piece of furniture—say, a couch—you assume that designers are keeping certain practicalities in mind when they produce it. Like the dimensions of standard doorways. I mean, why would someone create furniture no one can get into their house? My point exactly. Naturally, in the showroom, you're all excited with your soon-to-be new acquisition, upon which you'll spend many comfy hours watching TV or napping or cuddling the grandkids. As you hand the sales guy your credit card, it never occurs to you that you won't be able to get that honkin' big couch through your door.

Well. John and George hauled our couch to the slider, gave up, then plodded around another corner to the front door. Struggling in the soaking rain, they turned the couch upside down, sideways, backwards and forwards. Still, that couch resisted entering our home.

Propping one corner of the couch on the steps, John and George stood in the downpour, rain dripping off their ball caps, looking done for. I had to relent. I spread a fresh black swathe of plastic over the carpet, and in stepped John. We each grasped a corner of the couch, gritted our teeth, and as George pushed from the doorway, between the three of us we yanked, wrenched, and literally forced that beast inside.

Collateral damage included a big scar on the door frame, another one on the front of the door, and several mud spots on the carpet. But you know, "not sweating the small stuff" is perfect for times like these. Because we now had a couch in our living room (although it will probably need to be sawed into pieces when its usefulness is over and needs to be removed), instead of the alternative: that our couch would spend its final days residing in our muddy front yard, or sit in our garage until the end of time.

42 🦋 Boomers in the Boonies

There's living in the country...then there's really getting away from it all.

One of my mother's friends had gone on walkabout to the Far North—to grizzly country in the Alaskan bush. He lived in a beat-up cabin sixty miles from the nearest humans, with only an aged Volvo wagon for transportation. But as my dad used to say, "Let's not and say we did." Thankfully, John and I had been able to find this Foothills haven only an hour out of the city, without having to give up our family, friends, or life as we've known it.

The day after our move-in, the near-disasters with the couch and mud a fading memory, the monsoon was over. The sun peeked through the clouds, and seemingly overnight, spring had arrived. I opened the sliding glass door and inhaled a lungful of country air, the light and warmth like a balm on my face, then gazed around me. The newly-opened buds on the alders and birches created a lime-green mist that softened the landscape, and birds warbled happily amidst the trees and brush. As I closed the door and headed for my laptop, the quiet—aside from the drone of the flies and Garrett's hammering—seemed miraculous, the city racket of power-mowers and leaf blowers blissfully absent. Really, I could've kicked myself for not leaving town a lot sooner.

Now that John and I were officially county folks, we just knew we were made for boonie living. We embraced simple, old fashioned things. If there was a "Simple Living" scale, and Paris Hilton was a "1" and an Amish farmer in the Ohio heartland was a "10," we were a six…or maybe even a six-and-a half. Sure, I'd needed to make some initial adjustments at our new place, but I knew we could happily work our way up the scale.

For us, being retro is fun, like when John ignores the dishwasher to do the dishes by hand. Although I find this habit a little incomprehensible—especially when he bypasses the scrubby sponge and scrapes his plate with his thumbnail—he says it's a Zen thing, being in the moment and all that. When it comes to baking, I bypass mixers and bread-making machines—really, elbow grease and a halfway decent kneading technique are all you need. (Not like in movies, where people kneading bread squish the dough a little, add a pat or two and they're done.) And food processors, for cutting vegetables? Please. Our cars date from the mid-90s too, so we use actual keys to unlock the doors, instead of a remote control key fob.

Surely the plain black woodstove dominating our living room was simple living personified. (Though we hadn't actually fired it up yet. Since we didn't have any seasoned firewood, and living on a veritable firewood ranch, didn't want to buy any, we decided to wait until fall.) All in all, low-tech would be our mantra.

Our goal turned out to be more reachable than we'd figured… because we didn't have phone service. While we had every intention and expectation of getting it, the phone company had been unable to give us a solid date when we *would* have a dial tone. Aside from the inconvenience, I actually kind of…*liked* not having a phone. You're probably thinking, well, duh, she just used her cell phone. But surprise!—we didn't have a cell phone.

Nor did we want one…yep, we were cell phone-free out of choice.

Years ago, John and I decided we didn't need a cell. In fact, we liked bucking the everybody's-got-one trend, and making or taking phone calls anytime, anywhere, held no appeal. With our first visit to the property, Rick the Realtor had let us know wireless reception in the area was either very selective or non-existent. So we had an official excuse to stay wireless-less.

Going online at our new place would be low-tech too (that is, as soon as we got our phone service), since there was a fair-sized mountain between us and the nearest broadband service area. For us, dial-up wouldn't be a big deal either—we'd had it back at the old house. Meanwhile, I could justify not doing e-mail. Down the road, "when we had more money," we could always look into satellite Internet. I was prepared for the satellite thing to be an imperfect science, like area cell phone reception, but we'd worry about that when the time came.

You could, however, get cable TV out here—via satellite as well. John and I weren't tempted, since we agreed with legendary TV producer Fred Allen who said, "imitation is the sincerest form of television." Sure, Mom's monster TV and 300 channels had been fun while they lasted, but who needs TV when you're living your dream?

43 ❧ Walden Revisited

Our place is eight miles to the nearest village. A lot of towns this small are either a slowdown on a highway, or a place everyone but the old folks have left. But this one is a bustling little community of maybe two hundred residents, with a hybrid kind of look that's part New England, part Swiss Alps. Even if the picturesque atmosphere doesn't draw you in, a couple of restaurants, a gas station/convenience store, a mom-and-pop grocery, a liquor store, and teensy library make it worth your while to visit.

The mom-and-pop has an organic bent, with more personality than Regis and Kelly. It's staffed by an interesting microcosm of the village itself, from hippies to outdoor enthusiasts. They always look happy, and appear to be friends with all the customers. You can buy beer, rent videos, and get milk and eggs from farms right here in the county. They've also got more chocolate for sale than in Switzerland.

Our first week after moving in, we still had no phone. But with many, many calls to make to get ourselves organized, I'd take regular bike trips to the village. First, I'd stop in at the mom-and-pop for an imported candy bar, then cross the highway to the pay phone. The routine, along with our phone ring-free home, had a lovely kind of simplicity to it.

As the days passed without a working phone, however, I was starting to get a little annoyed. The simple life is all very well, but when you're getting caught in the rain on your bike, using a phone booth that seems to be grungier every time you visit (and don't you hate those icky handsets touching your head? You don't know where they've been!), then tossing endless quarters down its gullet, you can really appreciate one in-house. True, John and I were jonesing for the low-tech life. But since land-line phones have been around for more than a hundred years, I figured we could allow ourselves that modern convenience and still be old-fashioned.

The real challenge to lining up boonie phone service is keeping your psyche intact. If you don't have an inferiority complex already, calling the phone company over and over to nail down a connection date will give you one. You realize The Phone Company has absolute power, and you have…well, none. You have to go through their endless voicemail, and are forced to use speech prompts their friendly, automated woman "hears" only about fifty percent of the time. When you finally get a real, live person, they ask *you* questions, about technical issues like cabling and pedestal locations that *they* should know already. But each pain-in-the-tush phone call, I told myself, would bring me closer to not having to use this phone booth.

I had an even more powerful motivation for visiting the pay phone. Although I didn't keep moldering stacks of *The New York Times* around like my dad, I was hooked on the daily Seattle newspaper. Even at Mom's, I'd eschewed the news on her big TV, with its talking heads and crawls and alarmist stories about catastrophic weather and lurid murders. I know, the same content is in the paper. But it's easier to avoid, plus the paper is full of neat little human interest stories that don't make it into TV news because they're too busy covering the latest Britney/Lindsay/Hollywood Starlet of the Month meltdown. Give me a cup of Red Rose tea and a traditional newspaper to rattle and I'm a happy camper.

Once we'd unpacked, I figured I'd gone long enough without my paper. Time to restart my subscription. I pedaled down to the grimy booth again and surrendered my fifty cents. Upon reaching the circulation department, I blithely placed my order.

"Can you repeat your address?" There was a long silence at the other end of the line. "It looks like that's outside our service area."

"Outside your service area?" I echoed. They were saying I couldn't get a paper delivered out here?

The rep must have sensed my dismay. "Let me check on that." He put me on hold.

I'd have liked to think he was asking around the office if they could make delivery happen a few measly miles into the country. More likely, he was sharing a good old yuk with his co-workers, that some delusional customer wanted home delivery in the back of beyond. When he got back on the phone, he was apologetic. "It seems there aren't enough people in the area to support a motor route."

"Oh," I said, stricken. Then he said, "But mail delivery is available."

Why didn't I think of that? The Promised Land was at hand! Of course, it was probably a bit more expensive than delivery, but my newspaper was worth it. "How much will that be?"

"Just a sec—I've got to switch screens." In a minute, he was back. "It'll be $135 a year."

Gak! I managed to choke down an instinctive *are you nuts?*, thanked him, and hung up.

So my happy-camping days were over. I lived too far out in Boonieville to get the only newspaper I cared to read. It wouldn't have been so bad if I could buy my daily paper at the village Mom-and-Pop store, but all they could get was the Sunday edition.

I told myself there's a certain freedom in not keeping up with current affairs, except what happens on Saturdays, which isn't much. For now, communication with the outside world would be limited to going online at the tiny village library, and Garrett our contractor.

Garrett and his daughter took another few days to wind up the site prep. Once they'd put the finishing touches on the entry steps, they moved on to covering up the exposed home foundation. Garrett did the main earth-moving with his dozer, then Deborah hand-shoveled the dirt up against the concrete. As she worked, we chatted through my office window about her plans to get a job after graduation, then study overseas. No doubt about it, this Carhartt-clad Supergal—who could simultaneously work construction and attend college full-time—would go places.

With the foundation work done, our home looked like a real house now, instead of a big long box on cinderblocks. Garrett's final chore was leveling the rest of our half-acre, which naturally created more ruts, but now the place resembled an actual yard, and not a construction site. When I heard the dozer shut down, I left my desk to admire the result.

Instead, as I reached the front windows, I stared outside with dismay.

44 🐛 S'more Wood

John's got an old police saying: "Messy yard, messy house."

When you're an officer approaching a stranger's abode for a service call, it's best to prepare yourself for any untoward sights and smells. With the state of our yard, I was sure any stranger would conclude the inside of our house would be well, unspeakable.

I tracked John down for a consultation. "Garrett's 'done?' But the yard looks terrible!"

He'd pushed a woolly mammoth-sized tangle of stumps, brush, and tree refuse only as far as the edge of our cleared site. Our living room now looked out on a veritable Pike's Peak of slash, as high as our house. Although Garrett had been so tried and true throughout these long months, I simply could *not* look at that unsightly mess for the rest of my natural life! "We've got to talk to him before he leaves."

Though John wasn't one to make waves, especially with Garrett, he gamely accompanied me to the dozer. "Aren't you going to...um, mound up all that junk in piles?" I asked Garrett hopefully.

"No, it's a berm," Garrett explained, gesturing proudly at the hump of wood. "It's the latest trend in site clearing."

"It's not going to get burned?" (Meaning, *you're* not going to burn it?)

But Garrett, remember, was a greenie. "That'll create a lot of pollution," he said firmly.

I tried to think of all the greenhouse gases we'd spare the earth by leaving the pile as is, but what can I say? It was *so* ugly. "Isn't there any other way to get rid of it?" I asked in despair.

"How about if I bulldoze it down the hill?" Garrett asked.

I was doubtful. That mountain of slash, just heaved right over the ridge? For me, with my mom's tidy gene, out of sight isn't necessarily out of mind. "I suppose it's worth a try," I said, trying not to sound sulky.

Garrett grinned, in a conciliatory way. "All those stumps will create habitat for wildlife."

Meaning more critters would create burrows down the hill instead of in our yard? Okay, I could live with that. Garrett fired the dozer back up, and within an hour, he'd pushed the mound over the edge of our hill, to rest about twenty feet down the steep slope.

Quickest clean-up job I'd ever seen.

When I went back outside to thank Garrett for his dozing, I couldn't help pointing out to him—and to John too, in case he hadn't noticed—that we had several more brush and wood piles in close proximity. While they weren't anywhere near the size of the one we'd just gotten rid of, the fact the piles were *there* made me feel like a yard slob. "I think you can go ahead and burn those," said Garrett.

"Really?"

"Make a day of it," he said. "You can even roast some hot dogs or something."

"And some marshmallows," John said eagerly. "We could make S'mores!"

Later that day, I rode my bike down the road to see what the slash heap looked like from below, and you know, it didn't look half bad. In fact, if you squinted your eyes a little, the mess sort of blended in with all the other trees and brush and rotting logs.

The next day, Garrett's last, the whole gang came out to finish the site clean-up. Garrett, Gwen, and the kids had become like family—they'd been part of our project for nearly ten months. In that time, Gwen's braids had gotten longer, Garrett Jr. had started growing a goatee, and Deb's green bob had almost grown out—she was going natural for her post-college job hunt. The interesting hair aside, Garrett and his family had been like having your friends help you build your house—friends who'd made a dream happen.

At the workday's end, Garrett and his son loaded the bulldozer onto an oversized flatbed in Junior's charge. As the sun lowered in the sky, we said our goodbyes next to the family pick-up. Then John and I watched, a little forlornly, as Garrett, Gwen, Deborah, and Garrett Jr. climbed into their vehicles, then rumbled down the road and out of our lives.

45 🐛 House Calls

John and I returned to the real world a week and a half later, when the phone company finally connected our phone line. All too soon, the drone of the flies was drowned out by another, far more powerful buzz—a swarm of indoor contractors.

Our new home, which had received such a stellar grade on first inspection, now seemed to need frequent adjustments the way a creaky back needs chiropractic. If Garrett had been our outdoor house doctor, Mike, from Birch River, was our indoor one. He knew how manufactured homes work like an internist knows the human body. He'd stop by to make window or door tweaks, caulking or paint touch-ups, and plumbing or heating system attunements—all covered by warranty, thank *God*. And since a manufactured home is made with lots of plastic and formaldehyde (something I'd always known but upon buying one, preferred not to think about), Mike also strongly advised that while all this stuff outgases, you should keep your house ventilation fan on continuously—for the next *year*.

Given Mike's expertise, he seemed like the best person to ask about our murky water. "Put in a water filtering system," he suggested.

"That's not a bad idea," John said, but after Mike left, John and

I looked around our cramped mud/laundry room. "Well, there's no room for it in here," I said unnecessarily.

"We could put it in the pumphouse." John said, rubbing his chin. "But I don't think we really want to water the garden with filtered water."

Soon, Mike was spending so much time with us I thought I should start inviting him to family parties. After he'd tweaked everything that could be tweaked, in rolled Darren, Mike's co-worker, to diagnose a ventilation problem. We had an appliance guy over a couple of times to operate on the misaligned refrigerator door. A flooring guy arrived to make an incision in the kitchen linoleum to nail the sub floor to the beam. We had the Labor and Industries inspector dash over to examine the woodstove installation. Then a plumbing outfit pulled in for a second opinion on the ventilation. Really, our place was like a hospital ER.

Our off-the-beaten-track home was turning out to be a lot closer to civilization than we thought…only far enough out of town for all these folks to charge extra for the trip. And with all these comings and goings, it became clear that our mud room—our most convenient entryway—was misnamed. It was actually the *gravel* room. When you live on a gravel road, use a gravel driveway, have straw for sidewalks, and in fact, have no pavement on your property, you're doing a great thing for water percolation, but not for your floors.

We promptly instituted a no-shoes policy (well, I did, and John, being a good sport, went along with it), and most of our house doctors came prepared. But even with everyone leaving their shoes in the *gravel* room, a layer of grit would, quite mysteriously, creep off the welcome mat and migrate into the kitchen. Then, it would skulk a little further, onto our carpet, threatening to tarnish her golden locks to dull, dishwater blond.

Finally, the house attunements started to wind down, and one evening in late April, John and I convened at our dining room table. It was time to assess the damage.

46 🌿 The Money Pit

N ot to our new place, but to our pocketbook.
All those months at Mom's, John and I were confident that the extra equity we'd been able to pull out of our home sale would be plenty for our new life. That our fiscal eyes had been wide open. But a couple of weeks in the new house showed us what a fantasy we'd been living. How, we asked ourselves, did we end up with so many extras, not included in the original bid? With the final invoices rolling in, it was obvious we'd made our home-establishing budget with the optimism of innocents.

John and I received our first, minor financial shocker back in December, with the mini remote-control tractor that brought our house up the road. Apparently our home dealer had "forgotten" to tell us a day's work for the little robot thingy would cost $400. Maybe they figured we were either clairvoyant, or that if we wanted a house badly enough, we'd just shut up and pay. Well, we did.

I suppose I should have seen how our expenses were trending… and if this little financial ding was a warning, I hadn't seen it. Or I unconsciously ignored it. But who knew how the bare essentials could add up?

Take our nine months at Mom and Burl's. Even with rent-free digs, it's a long time to have everything you own in storage. And if you need three separate units, like John and I did? That'll be $1600, thank ya very much.

Then there was the electrical wiring for John's garage/shop. I'm not sure why we didn't think of it when we hired our pole building contractor, but I guess we were too busy fretting about the foot of rain we got the month he was working for us. And on top of the regular wiring ($1500), there was the *special* wiring for a future generator. Adding hundreds more.

What we'd bought for the inside of the house was an even bigger divot in our bank account. The appliances alone totaled $1800, and the cost of the woodstove was another $1800 more than the ever-so-attractive initial price of $999—making the grand total $2800. And the bill for our Marilyn Monroe carpet topped out at $3300. For the comforts of home, the rubber had met the road at over $10,000.

As the amount flashed before my eyes, like a sign in bright red neon, I felt a new flash of anxiety. How would we pay for the garden we'd been dreaming of?

Especially creating one out of a half-acre of bare soil? To start, we'd need tools, gravel, compost, and bark. Then plants. And more plants. Down the road, we wanted a fence, so we'd be plunking down even more cash for lumber, concrete, and wire. And every country place needed a tractor. As John and I compared our lists and bank statements, a light sort of went on, even if it was a low-watt bulb. We began to sense that life out here would be *far* more expensive than in town. The financial writing—like it had been when we downsized our house plans—was once again on the wall. Only it was graffiti: *The Simple Life Doesn't Come Cheap.*

Late that night, as John and I dispiritedly finished writing checks, marking "paid" on all the invoices and stamping the envelopes, we noted our remaining balance, and came down to earth with a thud. Disappointment like a weight in my chest, I squeezed John's hand. "I guess you know what this means."

John nodded, his face set. He could see as well as I could that the money for his dream office had vamoosed. There would be no cozy home-away-from-home for John inside the shop, no guys-only TV or microwave, no propping his feet up on a little potbellied woodstove, a cup of coffee warming on its top.

I looked out our kitchen window in the waning light, and knew the closest I would get to my barn was the red, metal-sided shop across the yard.

47 🦋 Slow Speed

With our bank account looking skimpier than a thong bikini, John and I resigned ourselves to dialing down our expectations.

Then one day, reading the newspaper—or was it in *O* magazine?—I stumbled across the Slow Food movement. Back in the 1980s, one Carlos Petrini and a bunch of his Italian compatriots created a huge brouhaha about McDonald's trying to muscle a new outlet into Rome.

Their passionate street protests attracted international media coverage. But news being a pretty ephemeral thing, the Romans' extreme objection to fast food was soon forgotten.

That is, until about twenty years later. Celebrity chefs like Mario, Giada, and Paula and the Food Network were hot, and suddenly, cooked-from-scratch food—especially Italian—was popular again. If this trend was all about simple and handmade, John and I could put a positive spin on our new, frugal-from-necessity country life. It would be like living the Slow Food way.

I suddenly felt more cheerful. But this SF deal had a definite learning curve.

Full disclosure: after a few days, I was going crazy without my daily newspaper. Buying the Sunday edition in the village (except when they ran out of papers before I could get there) was like getting a taste when I wanted a banquet. After days of angsting, I caved and ordered a far more affordable subscription to that nationally distributed newspaper I'd never really liked—you know the one, with bold colors on every page, heavy on fluff and light on substance. Reading it was like eating a Twinkie for dessert, when you really wanted wholesome pumpkin pie with real whipped cream, preferably organic.

The main drawback to taking the fluffo newspaper, though, was that I could collect it only on the days we went to the village for our mail, maybe every three days. Then I'd have the self-imposed pressure of catching up on all those papers, and knowing whatever I read would already be as stale as last week's bread. But at least I could follow what was going on with Britney.

Having a working phone again felt like we were in the fast lane… until we discovered there was something "special" about our phone line. In the parlance of the installation guy, the line had "interference" on it. Apparently that's some kind of resistance in the connection that means sounds aren't transmitted all that well. So voices sound fuzzy and indistinct, even a bit garbled. Talking to my with-it, Gen-Y daughters, I'm especially sensitive to sounding like an oldster, so having to ask them to repeat everything they say makes me cringe. Even if they're too polite to ask if I'm losing my hearing, I'm sure they're thinking it.

Our "special" line out here also meant that our dial-up Internet connection, that Ice-Age technology that is slow anyway, was absolutely glacial. So basic Web pages can take several minutes to load, and graphically-rich ones five times that. And don't even think about trying to download audio files, YouTube videos, or a good-sized PDF.

Other routines for the country life would take a 180-degree mindset switcheroo. Of course John and I had always known, at least intellectually, that we'd no longer have a ten-minute drive for almost everything—groceries, bank, doctor, and so forth—but an hour-long one. The reality of doing the driving and having to set aside an entire day for errands, however, came as sort of a shock. We learned to plan shopping and appointments with the strategic savvy of General Patton relieving the Bastogne, with every trip to town serving triple and quadruple-duty, if not more. While there's always the village mom-and-pop, they have a limited (and usually higher-priced) inventory. Clearly, living in the boonies would be all about making do with what's on hand.

That goes for entertainment too. We could rent a DVD, also at the mom-and-pop. But besides the cost of the movie, the two round trips to the village (pick-up, then drop-off) would take at least forty-five minutes out of the day. And if you're trying to be green, the half gallon of gas for the drive seems terribly indulgent. Renting, then, would be more of a rare treat.

All in all, the way things were looking, John and I would be hopelessly out of the loop. But when it came to feeding ourselves, we would be cutting edge. Slow Food, even if it was out of necessity, would be our default mode. Already, I missed the made-from-scratch pizzeria in town, and chocolate sundaes at the Dairy Queen. Without any take-out or deli nearby—or any fast food at all—meant that every night for us would be a Slow night. No break from cooking, dishes, or making sure we always had groceries in the pantry.

But ultimately, it was Foothills garbage management that crystallized what moving out here was all about—the Slow and Simple Life was really time-consuming. Instead of wheeling our bins down to the curb on pick-up day, we had to load them into the bed of John's pickup the night before and drive them a mile down to the main road. Then the next morning, it was down the road again to pick them up—the two trips making a total of four miles.

Maybe when the other lots sell and we have neighbors, we can carpool.

48 ❧ What's In a Name?

When you begin your new life in the country, your home and acreage will occupy your thoughts and conversations to the exclusion of everything else. And as you've seen, can also suck you financially drier than a daily trip to the casino. Given all the attention and money you're lavishing on your spread, it's a lot like having a new baby.

Clearly, you need a better descriptor for your place than "our place." Even if you have a simple manufactured home on a bare lot full of bulldozer ruts, and a rapidly depleting bank account, giving your property a name is an easy way to feel like landed gentry. Besides the psychological boost, John and I decided a name was just the inspiration we needed to transform our raw land into a rural garden.

As many have done before us, we decided to give our home a moniker relating to the landscape. And in our area, wild berries are the dominant feature: thimbleberry, salmonberry, and tiny strawberries, not to mention the pervasive—or shall we say, invasive—blackberry brambles. John and I easily agreed that any name we came up with should have "berry" in it. "Berryvine?" John suggested as we were clearing brush late in April.

"Hmmm," I said. "It fits, that's for sure."

We'd identified at least four kinds of blackberries, all in gradations of vine hazards. First come the native, low-growing kind that, except for our clearing, pretty much cover every inch of our acreage. The berries taste divine, and the thorns aren't bad. But the vines have this curious elastic quality, and an even more amazing ability to wrap themselves around your ankle and resist your every effort to pull your leg free.

A second variety is an upright blackberry that resembles a cultivated blackcap raspberry. Also very tasty, and the canes are at eye level so you can see them. They're probably the most user-friendly too, since the thorns are more inconvenient than dangerous.

Number Three in our blackberry spectrum is the Himalaya. Long canes, sharp thorns, yummy berries. They are worth the danger, but just because it's convenient to let this type grow near one of your pathways doesn't make it a good idea.

Variety Number Four, the non-commercial evergreen, is the most intrusive and yes, most lethal of all. The canes grow as thick as a man's thumb, with thorns like razor wire. They catch in your hat, gloves, and clothes, and as far as I can tell, will penetrate every fabric known to man except heavy leather. And if you're unwise enough to venture into the plant's vicinity with any skin exposed, the thorns will catch on *you*, leaving bloody runnels in their wake. The leaves are serrated and have thorns on them too, so in case you avoided getting trapped by the vines, the leaves'll get you. With the way Mother Nature often compensates for the dangers she puts you through, you'd think these berries would be the most fabulicious of all. But they're only, well, okay.

Dealing with these desperado plants, if you don't have a full set of motorcycling leathers, your safest bet is to dress in heavy denim, wear a hat and leather gloves, and have your mate close by. Because if the vines catch you in their octopus-like grip, you'll need someone to wrest them from your hat and clothes to set you free.

Looking at the red scratches on my hands from my last encounter with this demonic species, I said, "Actually, I don't think 'Berryvine' works for me after all."

So we were back to Berry "something." We mulled over the various geographical features of our area. "Berry Hill?" I said. "We're up on a hill, sort of."

Only there were loads of hills around here. Much bigger than ours—mountains, really—so "hill" wouldn't set our place apart at all. We toyed with more vegetation ideas. Berry Firs? No, berries and firs didn't have much of a connection, except that they were *everywhere*. Alder Berry? Alder trees were just as ubiquitous, and as a result, too many places around here were named Alder-something. Aldergrove, Alderwood, etc. Back to geography.

I had a sudden inspiration. "How about 'ridge?'"

"Berryridge," John said experimentally. He pulled a rotting log out of the weeds, and tossed it into our pile of brush. "I like it." With our home site perched at the top of a steep slope, our choice seemed the most apt. But Berryridge what?

That night, over dinner, John and I exhaustively discussed what the rest of our name should be. We seriously considered "cottage." But to me, a cottage is usually a gabled little affair with a thatched roof and mullioned windows, surrounded by a well-tended English garden with lots of foxglove and larkspur waving dreamily in the breeze. Not a box-like rectangle with nothing to soften the edges. Beside, we wanted to name our whole property, not just the house.

Could a name emerge from the crops we planned for our modest acreage? Non-lethal berries. Vegetables. Fruit and nut trees. We wanted to grow pretty much everything we liked to eat, at least that would grow in this climate. "Farm?" John said, his eyes twinkling.

"That's it!" Even if he was kidding, even if "farm" was a huge stretch, I didn't care. It's true, we had no immediate plans to raise critters, like chickens or cows. But we weren't going to simply dabble in gardening. John and I were going to grow as much of our own food as we could…enough to sustain us, and share the extra with family, friends, and the Food Bank. Plus I had a terminal case of barn envy.

As far as I'm concerned, that made us "farmers." And maybe one day, we could take off the quotation marks.

49 ❦ Garden of Eden

I think I was destined to be a gardener.

After Sunday school, in spring and summer, Dad would take my sibs and me to an arboretum on the banks of the Mississippi River. In the way kids focus on the obvious, we called it "Flower Park." To my eyes, everything about this lush, bloom-filled spot was magical, especially a pink flower with delicate heart-shaped blossoms. Each visit, I'd stop to touch the little hearts that dangled off the stem like charms on a bracelet. Then, after admiring the flowers and racing along the paths, my sister and I would tiptoe up to a mysterious little cabin half-hidden by shrubbery. We'd rattle the padlocked door, hoping that just this once, it would be unlocked (it never was). Full of delicious terror, we'd peer in the windows, sure a ghost or troll lived inside. Since all we ever saw was some faded old furniture, we'd give up, and head for the wishing well.

We kids would clamor for a penny, and after Dad pulled out a handful of change and parceled out one apiece, we'd make a wish and toss our penny into the water. I always asked for two things—that one day, I could get inside the cabin…and that we could have those heart-shaped, charm-bracelet flowers in our yard at home.

Although John and I were powerfully motivated to start our little "farm" as soon as possible, now, in early May, was too soon to put any veggie starts in the ground. My first priority, then, was creating something beautiful to view from the house. Besides, with our plans for food-growing, we needed to make our place as bee-friendly as possible. And what better way than to create my own mini-Flower Park?

But we had a lot to do before I could stick so much as a petunia into the earth. With our expanse of bare ground crying out for attention, John and I threw ourselves into basic landscaping. I'm a big reader of gardening articles, so I knew there was a right and wrong way to go about it.

When it comes time to install a brand-new garden, experts recommend—nay, insist—that you follow a certain orderly progression. First, you design it. Everyone knows this—a beautiful garden starts with a well-thought out plan. Maybe you even incorporate a garden *theme*. This of course, takes time, but you understand that all this planning and theme-ing pays off in the long run.

Once you've got your design in place, you can begin your hardscape: paths, retaining walls, water features, garden structures, and marking out planting areas as you go. Done properly, this step can take years, as you spend buckets of cash on wood and stone, and expend vast quantities of labor, your own and what you hire out.

Next, you create your beds. If your yard, like ours, suffers from bulldozer-abuse, you can either truck in topsoil, or simply force-feed nutrients to your resident soil—kind of like an overzealous coach pushes vitamins and protein drinks on a high-performing athlete. Only after feeding and amending the soil—a slow process, by the way, taking many months—then, and only then, are you allowed to actually put plants into the ground. Planting should follow a proper order too, starting with the most permanent, like trees and shrubs, then perennials, and last, your summer annuals.

Well, John and I were as impatient to get our hands in the dirt as a couple of science fiction geeks are for the next "X-Men" movie. We'd waited and longed for a garden big enough to grow whatever we wanted, and we wanted to do it *now*. So instead of the aforementioned process, we would go with our own ad hoc, quick-and-dirty method—plan, build, and plant as we went along.

Actually, our landscaping labors would be more dirty than quick; we were doing it all by hand. Since our mud/gravel room floor seemed to be a giant dirt magnet, our first task was building a gravel walk from the driveway to the door. For that, we developed a four-step M.O. Break ground for a path, rake it level, undergird the path with a layer of small rocks, then spread gravel over the rocks. The day John dumped the last wheelbarrow of gravel onto the pathway and raked it level, we stood back to admire the result, feeling like proud parents watching their baby take its first steps.

Civilizing that small stretch of ground (even if the dirt volume in the mud room was reduced by only about half) inspired us to keep our noses to the grindstone. We were multi-tasking mavens, simultaneously working on more paths, the beds adjacent to them, and our top priority, our orchard. As orchard project manager, John started a design for the layout and the fence, and he'd also be the chief coolie doing the labor. Meanwhile, along with all the other work we were doing, I began my personal perennial garden in front of our living room windows.

I also met my new best friend: the pickax.

50 🌱 Earth Mother

When it's time to install a garden, most people rent a Rototiller. But remember, our place was a former clearcut (and thus had never been tilled) in gravel-mining country. As we discovered the first time we sank a shovel into the ground, lurking just beneath the surface was a veritable morass of wood chunks and rocks…a morass that would only jam up a tiller.

Since John and I had to rely on sweat equity instead of a tractor, the pickax became our crucial landscaping tool. The site prep left us with severely compacted soil, which, exposed to sunshine, hardened to a consistency not unlike solid brick. So just like we had to bust up the ground for our first pathway, we had to do the same for our beds. For my project kick-off, I began hacking out a fifteen-by-fifteen foot planting area.

Given my Flower Park-loving younger self, you might think I was one of those precocious little kids who started a garden the first time I heard about Jack and the Beanstalk. Actually, I didn't pick up so much as a trowel until well after I hit thirty.

Inspired by home ownership—my first—and a featureless yard, I caught the gardening bug. The challenge: the builder had scraped away all the topsoil, right down to the hardpan. In my ignorance of proper planting techniques (and having no pickax), I adopted a kind of Stone Age method. I'd scrape out a hole that would barely fit in a plant's root ball, then after sticking in the plant, I'd fill in the hole with planting mix—aka, store dirt. Needless to say, nothing in that yard ever thrived.

For our new place in the Foothills, I had a vision of what true, natural gardening could be, encouraged by the gardening columnist in the Seattle newspaper. She didn't know me, but I knew her; she was USDA 100 percent organic. For sustainable gardening, she advises you to treat your soil as gently as puff pastry. If you have compacted soil, she suggests that you lay compost (organic, naturally) on your beds. Then on top of it, you add this stinky kind of soil tea you brew out of food scraps—and I imagine those scraps had better be organic too. You don't till your soil, or turn it over, because that will disturb the delicate microbial layers and biota. Besides, earthworms and other natural processes will loosen up the compaction for you. While you're at it, don't even think about stepping on your bed. If you must tread on the area, you're supposed to lay plywood on the ground and walk on that. Then, before planting, you must wait for your soil to rebound. Which can take years.

John pointed out two things: one, we didn't have that kind of time. And two, he wasn't donating any of his precious stash of plywood to sit in the mud, spoiling it for any other building uses. The only way we were going to get plants in our yard—for this growing season— was to break the soil up manually.

Since I wanted plenty of room for my baby plants' roots, I aimed for maybe ten square feet a day. Happily, I didn't have hardpan to contend with. Despite all the wood and rocks in our soil, it was a rich loam, loaded with organic material. Bulldozing had churned lots of that lovely loam beneath the surface (and sadly, must have smushed every earthworm into oblivion, because we never saw one). But once we pulled out the rocks, we had loose, nutrient-rich material to work with. So as a rank amateur, I grabbed the pickax to till my bed, one swing, one thunk at a time.

John is strong enough to lean over with the ax and just chop. But if you don't have a guy's upper body strength (I didn't), you've got to learn how to use every muscle to full effect. To wit: grasp the handle with one hand near the end and the other near the ax head. Grip it firmly too, lest centrifugal force causes the ax to fly out of your hands. Swing your arms back, then in an arc overhead, and on the downswing, use gravity by throwing your weight down along with the ax. A big grunt helps too. And do use the pointy end. The hoe-shaped side only provides more surface area to hit more rocks, which sends a painful reverb up into your wrist and arms.

Once you've buried the ax head as deeply as you can, rock the handle away from you to release the ax. If you're lucky, and it hasn't rained lately (a rare occurrence indeed, for spring in the Foothills), you can pull up your blade with only a little dirt clinging to it. If it has been raining—which is more often than not—a giant clod of soil will stick to the blade. That means more weight you've got to lift for the next whack, so you've got to knock the dirt off. You pull out the rocks you just exposed, or if you've hit a big one, you've got to toss your ax aside, and yank on it with both hands.

Then, once you've dealt with the rocks, you start in again. Grip, swing, throw down and grunt. Ladies, here's my top pickax advice: before you embark on country life, build your upper body strength. You'll save yourself many a backache.

Even though John and I were taking kind of a Boomer pace to this whole project, we still had aches aplenty. "I can't believe how much harder this is than ten years ago," John would say, panting as he carted gravel from one end of the yard to the other. Back in the day, when we landscaped the place in town, he could chop and hack and shovel all day long. Now, we were distinctly bummed to find our strength, endurance and "bounce-backability" was nothing like it used to be.

Still, by the middle of May, I had refined my ax technique enough to keep at it for an hour or two without collapsing. Just when I figured I could've won, or at least taken a Silver or Bronze in the pickaxing Olympics (that is, in a fifty-and-over category), I had to abandon my ax *and* my garden. It was time to leave for Sasha's wedding.

Leave Berryridge Farm.

51 Starry-Eyed

You'd think we'd be glad to get away.

Our bone-hard work in the yard was dusty and exhausting. Each task, each project we took on only seemed to germinate ten more, like those "Johnny jump-up" weeds that if you're dumb enough to touch, shoot seeds out in every direction. After sunset, when we ran out of photons, John and I would stumble into the house, almost too tired to make dinner. But I couldn't imagine leaving. Not this place, that in a few short weeks had become so beloved to me…

Some days, living here feels like I'm in a dream. When I walk up our gravel road at dusk, I encounter a perfect stillness. If there's no wind, and the unseen forces that make dogs bark or planes fly overhead are lying low, I'll stop, just to listen to the quiet. There's not one sound. Not the rustle of a leaf, nor the whisper of the fir trees. Nothing. The only sound of silence is the high harmonic in your ears, the ever-so-faint buzz that must be your neurons working or brain synapses or something. This stillness is the blessed, unworldly quiet that is a rare and precious commodity in our fast-paced, hurry-up world.

And on a clear night I can step out on my deck and see the Milky Way. Not just faintly sense where it is, like I did for years, but actually see that river of stars sweeping across the night sky. When I hear about corporate types who want to put advertising in space, beam up some commercial message to help line their pockets, I feel sort of violent. The night sky is priceless, and to lose that, we could lose our own souls.

52 ❦ Amtrekkies

"It matters not where or how far you travel, the further commonly the worse, but how much alive you are." —Henry David Thoreau

One sunny May afternoon, we departed for California, leaving the stars and the silence.

We were also leaving a multitude of projects undone or hardly started. But Berryridge Farm, for the first time, had to get plunked onto the back burner. Driving away was as painful as the day I'd waved goodbye to my daughter Meghann the previous October, as she stood on the porch of her little house in Oregon. She'd held her newborn son in her arms, tears rolling down her cheeks. Just as I'd kept my eyes on her and little Seamus until they disappeared from sight, I filled my gaze with the great hulk of the mountain facing our place, for one last glimpse.

Since getting homesick even before you leave home is no way to start a trip, I focused on what was ahead. If John and I weren't big on travel, we were especially *not* keen on flying. Not for us, whizzing through the sky in an aluminum tube at 600 mph. Instead, we were going to Sasha's Santa Barbara wedding via the slow-poke mode, Amtrak. John had taken the train to Phoenix five years ago and had loved every minute of it, and I looked back fondly on my own childhood train trips, so choosing Amtrak was a no-brainer. (And if you're trying to shoehorn your carbon footprint into a smaller size, travel by rail is far more fuel efficient than by air.) It's like satisfying your hunger with Slow Food. The train will take far longer, but you'll get to your destination in a more natural, human-friendly way.

Once we arrived in Seattle, the first leg of our journey was taking a taxi to Union Street Station in Pioneer Square. In the movies, you always have a slightly mad foreign taxi driver who talks a mile a minute, most of it incomprehensible. We got a Sikh fellow who said maybe two words the entire thirty-minute trip. We tried to be polite, you know, make conversation, but I got the impression we were imposing on the guy. Perhaps silence was how he maintained some inner peace, spending all day in Seattle's almost-permanent rush hour traffic.

The train station was in the middle of a decades' long remodel, to restore its former turn-of-the-century glory of granite walls and soaring ceilings. At this stage, however, the interior was dark and depressing, with a press of people milling around. Craving the outdoors, I stepped outside for a walk around the block, but my boonie sensibilities were more than a little rattled by the bustling traffic and pedestrian-filled sidewalks of Pioneer Square.

It was a lovely part of the city, though—Victorian-era buildings everywhere, with elaborate brick facades, crannies, and alcoves, all of which seemed to house coffee shops. I counted three (a Starbucks, Café Umbria, and Zeitgeist in one short stretch of Occidental Street), and everyone I saw clutched a coffee cup. I wondered if the efficiency people have sacrificed—living life one-handed so they can carry their coffee wherever they go—is compensated by all their extra coffee-fueled energy. But I was out of gawking time. I had a train to catch!

I hustled back into the crowded, noisy station, echoing with all those garbled announcements on the PA system you can never make out. But at least the sea change from quiet Berryridge Farm made it easier to put my old life aside and enter into the new world of travel. Besides, this trek was sort of a landmark for John and me...our first big trip together, after nearly twelve years of marriage. And my first train ride since 1977.

Judging from the line forming, we interpreted the gobbledy-gook coming out of the PA as the call for boarding. Excitement filled me as John and I climbed up the steps, at the front of the line with the other sleeper car passengers. Being ticketed for a sleeper means you're sort of the train "elite." That is, not one of the steerage class—I mean, coach passengers—who have to wait their turn until the upper echelon gets on. True, we didn't have a first-class berth, where you actually have your own teensy bathroom. But we'd gone all out (for us, that is) with a "roomette."

A roomette is about as small as it sounds, but I found it hugely more comfy than coach air travel. The seats feel acres bigger than airplane ones, wide enough for your average bum and then some. The beauty of a roomette is the privacy. You have a curtained door, and for sleeping, an actual bed. Okay, the bed's about as roomy as an MRI chamber, but still. You get to sleep lying down. While a roomette is not for the claustrophobic, John and I had lived nine months in our jam-packed little bedroom at Mom's. So we were good for this four-by-seven haven.

This train ride promised to be worlds away from my previous one. Seven months pregnant, I'd ridden coach with my eight-year-old sister, whose pleas to play King's Corner all day long were almost as insistent as the pain in my back from sleeping sitting up.

This time around, once we settled into our little nook, I felt cuddled in the lap of luxury. The roomette door was surprisingly soundproof, and you could surround yourself with all the comforts of home: books, magazines, and of course, snacks. You couldn't move around much in your roomette, but you could stretch your legs ambling up and down the sleeper cars…and thus avoid one danger of air travel: getting deep-vein thrombosis from sitting too long.

If you're looking for the Slow Life, you can't do much better than Amtrak.

If you like foreign films, you've probably seen lots of characters on trains. Tunnels and landscapes whiz by, and people get from Paris to Amsterdam, or Tokyo to Kyoto in about ten minutes. However, Amtrak's Coastal Starlight is no bullet train. You'll make anywhere from zero to fifty miles an hour. And why the dawdling pace, you might ask? Train tracks in the U.S. are often not that well-maintained. Plus passenger trains don't have their own separate tracks, so Amtrak must lease tracks from freight trains. Guess who gets priority? Yup. When a freight train needs a stretch of track, the Amtrak one must pull off onto a siding, and just hang out until the other train passes.

These delays happened frequently. At least every couple of hours or so. They'd generally last anywhere from twenty minutes to an hour, or even longer. Just like with construction delays, you'd find yourself completely at the mercy of forces beyond your control—in this case, the Gods of Burlington Northern.

So going by car, bus, or even dogsled is *way* more efficient...but once you accept the fact that your journey is as important as your destination, train travel is a blast. The chance to get outside for a few minutes at the major station stops means a bit of fresh air, and when it's time to jump back on the train, Amtrak porters really do bellow "All Aboooaard." (Unlike with the station PA, you can understand them perfectly.) Included in your roomette fare is an afternoon wine tasting with cheese and crackers, and even sit-down meals.

With space at a premium, you don't get your own table, like in a restaurant; instead, tables seat four, "family style." In the real world, eating with strangers would be last on my list of dining options. But surprisingly, meals turned out to be the highlight of the trip. It wasn't the food. It was the people you'd meet.

Have you ever noticed that once you're open to serendipity, happy coincidences occur all the time? With several cars full of passengers as potential dining-mates, out of our five onboard meals, John and I just "happened" to be seated with the same couple for three of them. They were the loveliest seniors from New Zealand, Cyril and Betty. Betty was the quiet grandmotherly type, while Cyril was the talkative one, with lively eyes and warm smile. He had a prominent, beaky nose, which gave him a slight resemblance to Big Bird. Whatever the topic, he had an endearing way of cocking his head and leaning forward, like he was riveted by whatever you were saying. He was probably a bit hard of hearing, but the gesture made you feel like you were the most fascinating conversationalist on earth. Energetic and adventurous, with open, questing minds, they'd come to America to bicycle around San Francisco and Denver. Back in our roomette,

John and I agreed that to make a long-term go of Berryridge Farm, we couldn't do much better than emulate Cyril and Betty.

Despite the delays, I loved the train. It became its own little world, a timeless place, where all you need to do is relax and eat and look at the forest and mountain vistas. The steady rocking had a hypnotic effect too. That night, we repaired to our cramped bunks, secure in the knowledge that we would wake up halfway down the coast of California.

53 ❦ Do the Locomotion

I awakened late that night, disoriented. Not because I was in a strange bed. It was that the train wasn't moving.

Okay, we'd stopped on the tracks many times that day. What made this stoppage different was that the entire car was in complete darkness. The kind of darkness that accompanies a power outage.

I sensed my bunkie below was awake too. "What do you think's going on?" I asked John sleepily, who as the son of Mr. Fix-it, is the resident Keeper of All Mechanical Knowledge. Not being clairvoyant, he hauled himself out of bed and went in search of a porter.

John returned shortly with the skinny. We were still in Oregon. And the train wasn't stuck on the tracks to let a freight train go by, but was experiencing, as they say, "technical difficulties."

Translation: a complete breakdown.

It was a long night. No electricity. For potty calls, you'd have to stumble down the hallway in the dark. And without running water, you couldn't flush, take a shower, or even wash your hands—which, for a germ-watcher like me, was almost as hard as not having working toilets.

Morning came, and we were still dead in the water. Or shall we say, dead on the tracks. After eight hours without power, the toilets were really icky—the stench filled the railcars, and without any ventilation, the hot, smelly air felt almost too foul to breathe. But in a perverse kind of way, the shorter delays the day before had prepared us for this longer one. And to give the Amtrak folks credit, they tried to maintain a sense of normalcy. No hot breakfasts, but the staff dispensed fruit and cold cereal, plus plenty of bottled water. (Not that I would use it to wash my hands, though I was tempted.)

Besides, our situation was nothing like the recent airline horror stories, with passengers stuck in planes on the tarmac and not allowed to deplane, not for food or water, much less to change a baby's diaper or let a toddler run off some energy. This morning, we Amtrakers had the freedom to climb off the train and into the May sunshine. The train had died next to a pasture, and while I strolled in the grass alongside it, some of the other folks got out their smokes, or on their cell phones to vent about the delay. Others periodically quizzed the porters on the latest developments—not that there were many.

By mid-morning, I was getting the feeling that my timeless little train world meant that I'd be stuck here in a field in southern Oregon forever (not counting occasional forays to the disgusting toilets). Then someone spotted a train engine tooling toward us, gave out a shout, and our motley bunch in the pasture began to cheer. Salvation!

We didn't get moving right away; disconnecting the dead locomotive and hooking up the new engine took another hour. But soon, the electricity was back on, the toilets up and running. (Not cleaned, however—I guess it wasn't in the porters' job description.) Somehow, though, the magic had gone out of the trip. Which could have had a lot to do with the smell of the bathrooms.

The glorious views of Mt. Shasta kept us entertained for an hour or so. But not enough to make us forget we were scheduled to arrive in Santa Barbara early that evening. We'd planned to check into our hotel pronto, get a quick shower, then race to Sasha's rehearsal dinner.

At 6 p.m., however, we were still in Northern California—with yet another delay. Apparently the engineer had gone over his twelve-hour drive limit, and another one had to be trained in. By ten o'clock, we'd made it only as far as Sacramento. And here we were with hotel reservations—pricey ones at that—in Santa Barbara, far to the south, for that night. Now, forget "low tech and proud of it"—what wouldn't we give for a cell phone! Somehow, we had to contact the hotel before they gave our room to someone else.

As the train chugged to a stop at the Sacramento station, John and I dove off to find a pay phone. Although we had ten minutes before the "All Aboard" warning, this station was immense, far bigger than Seattle's, and underground. Following the hoards of people, we raced through a vast, cavernous concourse that looked like an empty parking lot. Fortunately, John and I arrived in the main part of the station a few steps ahead of the crowd, helped, I think, by my previous incarnation as a race-walker. Searching wildly around, we located a bank of phones—and one was free. Thank God! With shaky fingers, I called the hotel hosting the wedding party.

"Our train's running late," I said breathlessly to the desk clerk, "but we want to keep our reservation." After some confusion (in another one of those coincidences, Sasha's mom and I share the same name), she confirmed we still had the room. The $185 per night room we wouldn't be sleeping in. As I hung up, I discovered we had two minutes to get back to the train.

If John and I had rushed into the station, we sprinted back out, our fifty-something knees rebelling with the abuse of trotting over concrete. My heart pounded, not just from exertion, but the fear that we'd miss the train.

But with seconds to spare, we got on board, then crawled into our bunks for a second, unscheduled night in our roomette. That night and the next morning, as more delays ensued, our regret and annoyance at missing the rehearsal dinner morphed into a new fear. That we'd miss Sasha's wedding altogether.

Had we made this one thousand mile, two thousand dollar trip all for nothing?

By breakfast time, the train's *click-clack, click-clack* had worn a groove into my brain.

Heading down the coast of California, John and I could see sparsely vegetated cliffs and glimpses of the Pacific Ocean...but no sign of a major city. And while serene and inspiring, the scenery didn't do much to stave off our nervous jitters—the wedding was only hours away.

You know when you're riding with a really slow driver, and you find yourself pressing your foot on an invisible accelerator, in an un-conscious attempt to get the car to go faster? I could feel my whole body sort of leaning forward, as if willing the train to pick up speed. But the train still chugged along at a jaunty little pace…clearly, not to be rushed.

So it felt like a miracle, when just after 10 a.m., the Coastal Starlight pulled into Santa Barbara. Travel-weary but jubilant, John and I de-trained, sixteen hours off schedule. With not a second to spare, I popped out the wheelie on my suitcase, then the two of us bundled our garment bags and carry-ons onto our shoulders for the three-block walk to the hotel.

I felt like a Sherpa packed for a climb up Mt. Everest. My arms trembled with the weight of all the luggage, but I could hardly pass anything to John. He was already hauling more than he could handle. "Whatever exercise we missed on the train," I said, gasping for breath, "we're sure getting it now."

54 ❦ "Goin' to the Chapel"

In another life, Sasha was probably French.

John's daughter has a certain *je ne sais quoi*…you know, that seemingly effortless way of doing things with style. She can twirl her blond hair into a roll, stick a pencil into it and look fabulous, or create a "homemade" gift that looks like it came straight from Williams-Sonoma.

Sasha brought the same flair to her wedding. It wasn't in a church, but at a state park several miles out of the city, high on a bluff above the Pacific Ocean. Artfully landscaped with trees, shrubbery, and stonework, the park was a balm to my outdoors-starved soul. As John and I walked up to the wedding site, a small amphitheater in the park, I breathed in the sea air gratefully. Despite the lovely location and Sasha and Sean's organizational skills, there was a glitch. As the clocked ticked closer to the starting time, we learned Collin, John's son and Sean's best man—in fact, the couple's sole wedding attendant—had gone missing.

In an interesting twist, at our own wedding, Sasha had been my bridegroom's only attendant. At the time, Collin had been in the

Marine Corps, and his unit had just been called to Haiti. So Sasha's role had been what John called Best Maiden.

Today, Collin had apparently showed up an hour or so ago... then disappeared. Generally, when a wedding is late, you can feel the attendees sort of tense up en masse. But this gathering was so laid-back—no tuxes, bevy of frothily-gowned bridesmaids, or frou-frou—you got the impression the delay simply provided extra time to enjoy the ambiance. Sean couldn't have looked more relaxed as he chatted with his dad and cousins, while off to one side was a trio playing soothing Irish ballads, guaranteed to induce calm. Still, when Collin at last made his appearance, you could sense the collective sigh of relief rippling through the crowd.

As it turned out, Sasha's bouquet, that crucial bridal accoutrement, had gotten separated from the other flowers back at the hotel and forgotten. Once a Marine, always a Marine, I guess, because Collin, in true "Semper Fi" fashion, had raced off to fetch his sister's flowers.

As the ceremony began, John, in his hastily donned suit, was every inch the proud papa as he escorted his only daughter to meet Sean and the celebrant. Sasha's simple *soignée* halter-gown fit right in with the rest of this unfussy celebration, and with her long hair in an updo, it was hard to imagine this was the same young woman as the rough-and-tumble collegiate volleyball player she'd been years ago. The non-denominational ceremony was surprisingly spiritual, and as I sat next to Sasha's sweet-faced aunt, listening to the touching, sentimental vows, I felt my eyes fill.

Afterward, in the break for photo-taking, I couldn't help comparing this gathering to my daughters' weddings. Carrie and Meghann had married young, at twenty and twenty-three respectively, and both couples and their friends had been in the "starter jobs" stage. When you have a twosome like Sasha and Sean, urbanites in their mid-thirties and well-established career-wise, your friends are going to be a pretty prosperous bunch.

Like the country mouse in the midst of city ones, I was quite dazzled by these yuppie Gen-X'ers, who somehow happened to be all very good-looking, all wearing an aura of success and confidence. Really, the whole bunch could have doubled as the cast of a chick-flick: the guys turned out in tailored suits and expensive haircuts, the young women bare-shouldered in their stylish outfits, despite the cool breeze. I wore my one elegant dress—well, elegant for me. It was pure silk, with long sleeves—actually a designer frock, albeit a cast-off from my wealthy aunt. Although I have nothing against hand-me-downs, and in fact, loved this dress, I felt like an escapee from Petticoat Junction.

All the women, even the ones my age, were bare-legged too, with open-toed high heels. After our chilly, rainy spring on Berryridge Farm, I wouldn't have dreamed of exposing my toes. I felt even more like a rube, with my plain, early nineties vintage pumps, and the only female wearing pantyhose. Later, my daughter Carrie told me that no one wears pantyhose anymore, it's all about bare legs. Well, I hadn't set out to make a fashion statement. And sure enough, I hadn't.

55 ❦ Weddings and Wakes

You think the success of any wedding reception rests on the food? The speeches? The free flow of Champagne?

Nope. It's the music. At Sasha's reception, on a flagstone-covered patio up a winding path from the amphitheatre, the Irish trio nearly stole the spotlight from the wedding couple. Once the food had been served, the band took center stage, and Will Quinn, the grizzled frontman, turned into the star of the show. Between sets, we struck up a conversation with Will, a real charmer despite his crumbly teeth and shaggy gray hair sticking out from beneath his newsboy cap. When John mentioned his surname, "Browne," spelled the Irish way with an "e," our man perked right up.

"Did you know there was an Admiral Browne, from County Mayo?" Will asked with a friendly grin. "He established the Argentine navy."

That impressed the heck out of John, an avid history buff. "So I could be related to an old-time celebrity."

"That's it," said Will, a County Kildare man.

"Wasn't the Marquess of Sligo, back in the 1700s, a Browne too?" I chimed in. (A factoid I'd picked up in my Irish novel-writing research.)

"Oh, yeah." Will's frown told me he was no fan of the Irish gentry (that is, your perfectly normal Irish person), making me think I shouldn't have mentioned it. Then I saw a gleam in his eye. "Have you heard the one about the two Irishmen marooned on an island?"

John and I shook our heads.

"Well," said Will, "the first one asks, 'Is there a government here?'" Like any halfway worthy joke-teller, he paused dramatically. "'The second one says, 'If there is, I'm against it.'"

We got a good chuckle, then Will was off for the next set. He played the pennywhistle and accordion, and also did all the stage commentary (the other two guys didn't say a word all afternoon). Despite his ratty looks, Will must've had a lot going for him. He'd brought three "groupies" to the wedding—his lovely Mexican wife Trini, and two beautiful daughters, Aoife and Bridgit. In their early teens, Aoife and Bridgit were competitive step-dancers. For this gig, besides their petticoated dresses adorned with Celtic knots, they wore full Irish dance regalia, from their curly-wigged heads (the desired step-dance look involves hair that doesn't occur in nature), to their soft-shoe encased toes. Aoife and Bridgit not only danced on stage, but provided back-up on the chorus of "Finnegan's Wake."

"…A bottle of whiskey at his feet," sang the dewy-faced girls, "And a bottle of port at his head." Then as Will took up the next verse, Aoife and Bridgit resumed step-dancing, which inspired the groom's boisterous Irish family to hit the dance floor.

I watched in admiration. This was the kind of close-knit Irish clan our family had never been. My family is more closet Irish (except for my Grandma Alice serving boiled potatoes for dinner every single night of her life). We kids all had Anglo-Saxon names, except for me (middle name of Colleen). But with Sean's family, every guy I met was the likes of Conor or Patrick, and for the gals, Sinead, Maureen, or Mary, hyphenated with Margaret/Alice/insert any female Irish name here. While my dad had been a complete teetotaler, Sean's family freely imbibed the fruit of the grape. My siblings and I had also been raised Presbyterian, despite my parents' Catholic wedding and a promise to raise their kids in the Church. Family dancing, by the way, much less the Irish kind, had never taken place beneath our roof.

But this gang had no such inhibitions. As Will picked up a rol-licking beat, the female contingent kicked off their fashionable heels. As I joined in the dance (keeping my sensible pumps on), I noticed one cousin, a comely young lass with red hair, and one of those very petite but *very* buxom girls, had gotten quite tipsy. Not to worry, though. She still had the presence of mind to lead a credible Irish reel, and when she went off track—that is, started dancing in the entirely wrong direction—another cousin would grab her and send her down the line.

Back on the sidelines sat one of the Irish aunts, holding court. With her well-coiffed hair, and wearing red-striped high heels, she reminded me of my Grandma Alice, the Hedy Lamarr look-alike—a faded beauty, exquisitely dressed. Although Grandma had died when I was sixteen, I sensed she never got over losing her looks. This aunt, though, with those flamboyant shoes, was clearly still in the game.

I'd never felt more Irish. Though I hated for the day to end, we would leave for home the next afternoon. Saturday night, God and Amtrak willing, would see us back on Berryridge Farm.

56 ❧ Ax and You Shall Receive

Without the anticipation of the wedding, the Amtrak trip north was flatter than week-old soda pop.

While the California coastline and the Cascade mountain views were just as breathtaking, John and I longed for our familiar land-scape. And feeling jumpy in our cramped roomette, I yearned to not only see wide open spaces, but be out in them. Yet, as we chugged the long miles toward Seattle—blessedly free of unusual delays, with only the usual ones—I realized I'd found a hidden blessing in our train experience. I was learning to "live in the now" (those Buddhists again). To let go of impatience or fretting about what lies ahead and just *be*. Even if *be-ing* on Amtrak, at this moment, meant being a good sport about arriving in Seattle three hours late.

On the drive home, way out in the boondocks, John and I passed a small church with a signboard out front. With a chuckle, I read it aloud. "'Is God your Steering Wheel or your Spare Tire?'" It was like country Zen wisdom or something. Since we'd apparently been "guided" to take the train, it seemed pointless, not to mention being very unBuddha-like, to regret the outlay of extra time or money we'd spent. Besides, John and I admit we'd still take Amtrak (even with the breakdown) over plane travel any old day.

After six days away, we pulled into our driveway, bursting with stored-up gardening zeal. Compared to the scenic grandeur we'd viewed from the train, our half-acre yard looked as naked as a newborn bird, save for the light fuzz of sprouting weeds.

My unfinished perennial bed beckoned with a siren's song, as if saying, "I've been waiting for you, Big Boy." (Make that Big Girl.) I rededicated myself to pickaxing—though after being away from Berryridge Gym for a week, I had to go easy with my out-of-shape axing muscles.

On my breaks, I'd mosey around the corner of the house to our new orchard site, where John was digging post holes for the deer fence. John and I were taking no chances with all the tasty, deer-tempting goodies we planned, like apple, pear, and hazelnut trees, and as many blueberry and cane berry plants we could fit in. We'd heard deer are prodigious jumpers, so you can't build just any old fence—it's got to be eight-feet high. And you'd better make it stout. (In case a deer tries to jump your eight-foot fence anyway, can't make it over, and crashes into it instead.)

That means sinking your posts good and *deep*. The trouble was, the soil in our orchard was just as compacted and full of rocks as the rest of the yard. And for some strange reason, there seemed to be a huge rock lurking right where each post was sited. The rocks, however, turned out to be no match for John—he's like a determined dentist with an impacted wisdom tooth. Using an array of tools—the pickax, shovel, and handfork—he would allow no boulder to defeat him, even if it took all afternoon. And sometimes, it did.

Instead of the crowded quarters and heavy clay of our garden back in town, the trees and berries we had in mind would surely thrive with our orchard's generous space and well-draining soil (that is, once you break it up). While John was always up for daydreaming out loud as we worked, mostly about a blissful future of bushels of apples or gallons of blueberries, I couldn't put off the inevitable forever. So with a sigh, I'd return to dirt pounding and wood-debris extraction.

Progress was slow all around, since on John's rock-mining breaks, we started creating some flowerbeds alongside our new path. But my labors in my big bed paid off. About ten days after we returned from California, I heaved my last stroke of the pickax, and finished raking the earth smooth. Lest you think I could now put plants in the ground, such was not the case. Next, I had to dig the entire plot with the spading fork, to unearth any rocks and wood junk I might've missed with the pickax, then rake it *again*. But my bed still wasn't ready.

For our little farm, I was keen to forgo chemicals. And I'd also heard that soil amendments in your garden are better than fairy dust. So John and I splurged on a truckload of mushroom compost, and for easy access, had it dumped next to the orchard. Why they call this particular product "mushroom" compost, I can't say, because it's really aged chicken manure. I never figured I'd be up for a heap of old chicken dung next to my house, but that was before our Amtrak trip. After you've had to use a yucky toilet for a day and a half (after paying dearly for the privilege, no less!), a bunch of manure doesn't faze you so much.

Besides, if chicken poop would help my fledgling garden, bring it on! After many wheelbarrow loads of compost to my big peren-nial bed, and more for our side beds, I spread it out, turned the compost into the entire area with a shovel, then raked it lightly one last time.

Now, planting could happen!

57 🦋 Flower Park: The Next Generation

Besides assiduous soil-coddling, the success of your garden de-pends on wise plant choices.

John and I brought our little plant refugees out of the orphanage behind the Big Stump, then wheelbarrowed them into the yard. Last summer, hauling all those pots from the old house to John's pickup, then from the truck to the stump, had seemed like such a big chore. But now, as we surveyed our paltry little stash, it was clear these few transplants would make a pretty sparse garden. And while the straggliest-looking specimens have been known to develop into stellar performers, why take chances? If we wanted lush, abundant flowerbeds, we'd have to go retail.

We headed to a Foothills nursery with a sterling reputation a scant dozen miles away (one that back in town, we'd always meant to visit but had never gotten around to). The stock was more expensive than what you'd find at the grocery store, but most of it was grown either on-site, or obtained locally or regionally. They also staffed their outfit with gardeners who seemed to have a Ph.D. in every plant on the premises.

Appropriating one of the nursery's flatbed wagons, John and I spent a heady hour filling it until pots threatened to fall off the edges. With hardly a lick of shade in our new beds, I couldn't grow bleeding hearts, the flower I'd loved back at Flower Park. But we'd make up for it with our bounty of bee balm, "Purple palace" and coral bells heuchera, crocosmia (two varieties), and day lilies. We also chose a cold-hardy heavenly bamboo, and lots of bee-friendly herbs like mint, sage, and lavender.

Besides our pots from the old garden and the nursery stock, our inventory included an unidentified plant Mom had given us that looked like a mint cousin. We had no idea what this Mystery Perennial was, but the plant-care stick was in the pot. *Reaches 18 inches.* Okay, it would easily fit into my big bed. And, *Ideal for dry, warm climate.* That hardly describes the Foothills, but the plant was free, wasn't it? John and I began planting our booty, finishing with the remaining ex-pats from our place in town, a honeysuckle sprout and a one-foot tall Japanese maple.

The final step for our new garden? Enjoying it.

Those quiet, uninterrupted interludes I'd anticipated, having a peaceful teatime in my mini-Flower Park, serenaded only by the sweet drone of bees, didn't quite pan out.

All was not perfection, here on Berryridge. With the acoustical disadvantage of sitting high on a ridge, we could tell other folks in the vicinity, unlike us, did not want for power equipment. The rumble of tractors and construction vehicles, and the whine of chainsaws drifted up to our place. And when the wind was right, we could even hear the gravel mining operation four miles away. Then on weekends, we got hammered by recreational racket—motorcyclists who treated the main road below like their own personal motocross route, producing a roaring buzz that sounded like a swarm of angry hornets.

And there was another kind of din—one we thought we'd escaped. While my mom calls our area "God's country," the Foothills, as I see it, are also "Gun Country."

With motorcycle noise, at least you know it'll quickly pass. Not so with gunfire. Which, as it turns out, was just as common around here as it was near the country estate properties we'd taken a pass on. There were no rifle ranges around here, you understand—only lots of shooting aficionados. One gun-lover in particular would start in around late afternoon, and often go until dark. He (or she) was at it so regularly John came up with a name for him: "Shooter Bob."

With firearms being John's former stock in trade, he'd assure me that folks weren't shooting *into* our place but *away* from it. I wasn't so sanguine. During the shooting sprees, I'd take a walk down the drive, wondering if a stray bullet would get me. One day, assailed by a solid five hours of Shooter Bob's gunfire while we worked in the garden, I sighed heavily. "Honey, this is really getting to me."

John stuck his spading fork into the earth to stretch his back. "I'd rather listen to guns than skateboarding," he said.

Who could forget the daily kerthumping at the old house, right across the street? Except I actually had. "Me too...I guess." I *guess* I'd take gunfire over skateboard-jumping. Either way, if this was "normal" country noise, I'd have to get used to it.

58 🦋 Unsolved Mysteries

But we also had what you might call *abnormal* country noise.
    The previous August, when John and I had played in our new woods, we'd seen no evidence of paranormal phenomena. But now, ten months later, we found a mystery brewing at Berryridge. Each evening, about an hour before sunset, a sound would commence that neither John nor I had heard before, a weird, electronic *twang* every

few minutes. It seemed to be right over our heads, but at the same time, come from nowhere. Unable to detect a trace of anything—animal, vegetable, or mineral—that could produce this odd whine, we were stumped.

"Bats?" John guessed one evening, as he was pickaxing and I was collecting rocks. Craning our necks, we examined the air above and around us, but except for some flies, saw no sign of airborne creatures.

"Woodland fairy sprites?" I wondered. "They're invisible." Okay, I was joking, but I knew someone who could "see" them. Tossing a few more rocks into my pail, I said, "How about government surveillance?" Given what we'd heard in the news lately, it didn't seem too far-fetched. But there were no planes overhead, and the brush that covered our whole area wasn't tall enough to obscure any suspicious equipment.

Each evening, as the confounding sound continued its reverb, we'd search the sky and exchange more theories. "Deer, like, calling to each other?" said John, on a pickaxing break.

"Like a whale song?" I pondered this with more rock gathering. The thing was, we saw all kinds of deer during the day, who didn't "say" a word. Maybe they were too busy eating to vocalize, but still. "Doesn't seem too plausible."

"Changes in atmospheric conditions," John proposed. "Some kind of unusual air currents among all these hills." Now that really *was* a stretch.

Then I said, "Aliens?" We laughed, then abruptly stopped. You always hear aliens only land out in really deserted locales. What with our isolation, maybe it wasn't so funny after all.

But whatever that puzzling noise was, we couldn't let it get to us. We had work to do.

Our first Berryridge visitors, not counting the house-doctors, weren't stray motorcyclists *or* shooters, but Mom and Burl. Taking them around our newly created paths and flower beds, John and I couldn't help preening a bit as they admired our progress. "Use Miracle-Gro," Burl advised, who spread it lavishly around their yard and flowerpots. "It's the best fertilizer around."

I admit, I was tempted; the flowers in their yard grew mutant-fast. But once they'd left, and the lure of Burl's Miracle-Gro dissipated, I privately resolved to stick with all-natural. Going slow, the point of living here, would have to do for our plants too.

When it comes to perennials, there's no point in being in a rush anyway. Most gardeners have heard the old adage, "First year they sleep, the second they creep, the third year they leap." Apparently, here in the Foothills, the combination of virgin soil (previously untouched by a trowel) and chicken manure worked like a shot of growth hormone. Our baby plants skipped the sleep-and-creep stage, and went directly into the leap.

A week or so later, I gazed out the window in near-rapture at our new beds, perennials pushing out rich June greenery, their flower buds plumper than a holiday turkey, and said to John, "Can you believe the way everything grows out here?" It seemed every bit as mysterious as that weird evening noise.

He ambled over for a look, and put his arm around me. "A lot faster than in town," he said, smiling back at me.

So imagine our consternation when we woke up one morning, and found our flowers' lush new growth had disappeared.

59 🌿 Deer Me

We'd been hit by dine-and-dash experts. They were the four-legged kind, not intimidatingly large but prone to extraordinary eating binges. The wily, black-tailed deer.

You may be thinking, doesn't "wily" imply a certain amount of intelligence? Of cunning? We've all heard the cliché, "like a deer caught in headlights," reserved for the most clueless. All right, it's true. Deer are dumb—but they're not stupid.

Back in town, with so much green space around, we'd see a deer here and there. Once in a while, you'd even catch one strolling down the sidewalk. I admired their graceful gait, gentle eyes, and their quietness. I especially admired the way the deer stayed out of our garden, especially since they had made free with our neighbors' yards. Needless to say, we weren't foolish enough to plant roses in our unfenced front yard.

In the Foothills, small herds of deer are everywhere—in the fields, on the roads, in the brush…and on our property. A doe with a solo offspring, as well as a mom and her twins were regular visitors. (Dads seem to keep vampire hours—we never saw hide nor hair of 'em.)

Given this animal's free run of our place, John and I had to get up to speed on deer-friendly ("Yum!") versus unfriendly ("Blecch!") plantings. First, we consulted all our gardening books, making exhaustive lists of the "Blecch" items. Then just to make sure, we'd run a smell test past the deer-savvy staff at the Foothills nursery. As in, "Will the deer eat this?"

"It depends," the clerk would say ruefully. "They'll try anything."

Sure enough, our Foothills experts were right. Daylily blossoms got deadheaded, and the new growth on our young maple trees a hard, lopsided pruning. The deer bit the entire top off a filbert sapling. To our deer visitors, the coral bells bordering our walkway were like kimchi to the Koreans. Mornings, I'd often arise to find an entire side of three or four plants munched down to the crown.

With all the six-foot tall fireweed—a deer favorite—that grew abundantly, nay, prodigiously all over our property, you'd think they'd leave our meager plantings alone. But *noooo*. They tried them all.

In frustration, I investigated natural deer deterrents. The main key to protecting your plants, I learned, is to permeate the areas around the deer chow with strong odors. My garden columnist mentor recommended decomposing sulfurous-smelling vegetables, like onions. Without a ready source of bulk onions, much less rotten ones, I focused on an alternative: human-related smells. (Any of you out there with delicate sensibilities may want to skip this next section.)

Human hair, for example, is apparently a great repellant. So every morning, after cleaning my hairbrush, I'd hang clumps of hair onto the boughs of the young maples. But the deer just nosed around the hair and kept eating.

I guess my all-natural shampoo didn't smell perfumy enough. Something stronger was required. So I tore the cologne ads out of my *O* magazine, the ones that have a strip of scent imbedded in the page that stinks up your entire magazine, and artfully arranged them around the foliage of our perennials. But the success rate was about the same as with the hair.

Okay, maybe these smells were too easily dissipated by the weather. I brought out the heavier guns. We tore rags into strips and soaked them in some of John's twenty-year-old English Leather aftershave (I told you he didn't like to throw anything away), and attached them to any plant the deer liked. And it worked…for a few days. Then the deer were back to their a la carte dining.

Our aggravation mounted. We'd had it with seeing new garden damage each and every day. John and I decided to pull out the really big artillery: our ultimate deer weapon.

At least it worked in the movie *Doc Hollywood*. Michael J. Fox plays a hotshot, big-city doctor, and through a trick of fate, he gets stuck in rural South Carolina, and falls for an environmentalist small-town girl. In one scene, she and Michael are out in the woods and stumble across a hideaway for deer hunters. Being a vegetarian and vehemently opposed to hunting, the heroine decides to take action to keep the deer out of range. She…well, pulls down her jeans and pees in spots all over the woods. And she gets Michael to do it too.

Well, I'm sure you can see where I'm going here. We had lots of privacy around the property, so John, whose operations are less cumbersome than a female's, made like Doc Hollywood and spread the joy wherever the deer were noshing.

Our deer friends must not have seen the movie. Because a little human urine didn't seem to bother them in the slightest. John and I had to conclude that *nothing* was safe. Except aromatic herbs like mint and lavender. Thus, our dilemma: we wanted to grow *real* food on Berryridge Farm. Other than a touch of *herbes de Provence* here and there, I didn't see us eating too much lavender. (To me, it would be like eating soap!) We faced the hard reality. If we wanted to feed ourselves from our little acreage, everything, and I mean *everything*, would need protection.

Safeguarding the orchard, John and I agreed, would pay off. We'd already witnessed how one neighbor had planted many dozens of apple trees, enclosing them in a *five*-foot fence strung with three rows of wire. Can you say, Bad Haircut? The deer stripped the entire field of young trees down to two-foot stubs. I'd also watched deer slip through our rancher neighbor's barbed wire fence as effortlessly as Jacob Marley walks through Ebenezer Scrooge's bedchamber door in "A Christmas Carol."

After many weeks of labor and gouges in our bank account, John had finished a take-no-prisoners fence around the orchard. He'd sunk eight and ten-foot 4 x 4 posts into concrete, strung four-inch utility wire, called steer wire, around the top half, then attached chicken wire from the ground to midway up the fence. Around the top, he wound a single strand of wire, giving the compound the faint flavor of a prison yard. But the rest of our place was still vulnerable. We planned to fence our entire half-acre one day, but that would take more time and energy and money than we had right now. So, determined to deny Bambi and Company the Browne Salad Bar, as much as possible anyway, John and I gerry-rigged a temporary fence around my treasured perennial bed.

It had a certain Rube Goldberg look, with birch boughs substituting for treated fence posts, and only four-feet high (that is, easily jumpable). But the deer stayed away. Well, why would they bother? In the rest of the yard, they had all the yummo, unprotected delicacies they wanted! As each day brought more damage, even their darn hoof prints messing up the beds, John and I would kvetch daily about our deer problem. "Where's Shooter Bob when you need him?" I'd grumble.

Yet...deer are such pretty animals. We couldn't help getting fond of them—sort of like the lovable kid brother who comes to visit and eats you out of house and home. They were so fun to watch too, especially the mom and twins who stopped in regularly. And who knew fawns could actually play tag?

Although you *really* wish they wouldn't play it around your new beds. John developed a new country skill—deer wrangling. If he was working inside when they wandered in (I think they were following a personal path they'd established long before we came) I'd yell, "John! Deer in the yard!" He'd jump from his desk and race outside, arms waving. Thankfully, these critters are easily spooked, and would leap back into the brush.

But do not be deceived by their gentle demeanor. Inside many a deer beats the heart of a lion. One day, as John was trying to herd the twins out of the yard, a small but gutsy fellow actually turned to confront him, planted his little front feet in the dirt, and stomped them defiantly.

John came into the house laughing. "I've been sassed—by a fawn!"

60 ❦ Flower Power

As the deer skirmishes continued, we bought more chicken wire.

No, we weren't building two-foot high fences. (The deer would probably get a stomachache from laughing at us, which would only provide a temporary solution.) Nor were we ready to raise chickens. We'd come to our last line of defense—protecting each plant individually.

While the deer ignored our herbs and bee balm, John fashioned little wire huts to protect the coral bells, sea pinks, and daylilies. And soon, just past the summer solstice, our newly safeguarded flowers looked like Burl had snuck in to spoon-feed them Miracle-Gro, with a riot of blossoms poking up through the wire. As clover began filling in the bare spots in the yard, its scent so strong and sweet you could almost taste it, in flew the kind of visitors that brings a glow to a gardener's heart.

In the afternoon's warmth, the drone of honeybees in our yard was like a symphony. A lot of folks are scared of getting stung, but really, honeybees are the most benevolent of creatures. I'm not quite up for letting the little guys climb all over me like some beekeepers do, until they look like they're wearing a bee sweater, but I'll often be weeding around a plant, with bees companionably working the blossoms only inches away. Somehow, they must know I mean them no harm.

And the butterflies! Back in town, butterflies were a rare sighting. (I put their increasing urban absence down to the use of Round-Up, Weed 'n Feed and bug spray.) But here in the country, butterflies of all kinds flutter everywhere, especially the larger Monarchs and a tiny, indigo variety. Besides these two pollinators, our place attracted more "good garden friends," as John calls them—the ladybugs. You gardeners know they eat aphids like deer eat coral bells. Back in town, John and I once purchased a nursery package of ladybugs and released them near an aphid-infested honeysuckle. Now, I have to laugh about actually *buying* them, because our place has turned out to be their breeding ground. On sunny days we'll see hundreds of ladybugs buzzing in the shop windows and climbing all over the house. Even if we weren't aiming to be officially organic, our close-to-natural garden must have been helping our little pals be fruitful and multiply.

Those low-key bugs, bees and butterflies, so in sync with the Foothills pace, were all very well for peacetime. With Berryridge in bloom, however, we were in the middle of a combat zone. It wasn't a war we were waging, like with the deer, but one we were watching.

John and I had hummingbirds back in the old garden, so we were familiar with their dive-bombing habits—part of their mating dance, or monitoring their territory, John guesses. Foothills hummingbirds, though, are the most comically aggressive ones we've ever seen. With so much space to protect, these little warriors engage in dogfights that rival the Red Baron's. Their rat-a-tat-tat chatter filling the air like machine-gun fire, they'll chase each other with breathtaking aerial acrobatics. You'll be out weeding, minding your own business, while they whiz past your head so close you can feel the rush of air past your ear. These hummingbirds don't only fight their own kind; one day I caught one browbeating an unsuspecting little sparrow into cowering under the deck. Rather than share the sage, with dozens of purple-spiked flowers up for grabs, they'll even chase honeybees away. Some people would rather watch a bunch of folks at each others' throats on "Survivor," but for John and me, this was way better entertainment.

Mom's Mystery Plant took to its new home as enthusiastically as our hummingbirds. Undaunted by our cool early summer, it quickly passed the eighteen-inch mark, and within weeks the pink blossom tips were as tall as my chin. Each evening, John and I would gaze with satisfaction around the garden—growing flowers in the Foot-hills looked like a pretty sure thing. But the real test for Berryridge was before us.

The "farm" part.

61 🌿 Bear Necessities

My vision of farming was all about living closer to the land—a connection that included composting our kitchen wastes. In our old garden, there was no room for a compost bin, but now we had ten acres! Plenty of room for a major composting operation, and we could locate it far enough away from the house so no untoward odors would smell up the yard. Surely the food we raised would thrive with our all-natural (naturally!), Berryridge-produced compost. Besides, when you have an on-site septic system, I understand using a garbage disposal will interfere with the decomposition process in the septic tank. All those food scraps, then, might as well be returned to the earth.

Those first couple of months, as we settled in, just thinking about my future compost pile, so green, so recycled back to Mother Earth, I felt a bit smug. But before I could cast so much as a carrot peel upon the ground, I learned the word on the street—or in the hills, in our case—is all about being "Bear-Smart."

You have "Bear-Smart" ads in the local paper, "Bear-Smart" stickers on your garbage bin, "Bear-Smart" flyers in the Post Office. Being Smart About Bears means keeping pet food dishes inside, storing your outdoor grill in your garage, and putting out birdfeeders at your own risk. And if you've got berry bushes or apple trees, you're supposed to pick up all your fallen fruit and dispose of it as soon as it hits the ground. Above all, you're advised to allow nary a shred of food waste outdoors.

Well, that sounded advisable, but I couldn't imagine bears being *that* close. Even if one of the locals prominently displays a homemade sign in his yard, *Beware of the Be*—with a giant cutout of a bear claw whacking off the "a-r." I figured, if bears were a real problem here, people wouldn't be joking about them.

Until the afternoon I was out on my bike, and about two miles from home I saw a big, black something lumber across the road about fifty yards in front of me. Hoo-boy. It was a bear all right. A real, live one.

I'd seen black bears before, in the wild. Well, sort of the wild. When I was fifteen, I visited a girlfriend at her remote cabin in Northern Michigan. Since we were too young to belly up to the local bar, and the nearest mall or movie theatre was at least a couple of hours away, we settled for the only entertainment around: bear-viewing at the all-you-can-eat community garbage dump. We watched from the safety of our car as these overfed Ursa majors dined in style. You could have dangled a salmon steak right at them and they probably wouldn't have blinked.

But here was proof that the Foothills had *real* wild bears. Bears looking for real food. This bear would be one of them. Not wanting to be bear-lunch, I cautiously rode forward, but it had disappeared into the brush. Maybe this sighting was an isolated incident? A bear had mistakenly wandered too close to civilization, but was immediately heading back to the wilderness, far, far away from our place?

Not long afterward, I was riding about a mile from the bear crossing. A car slowed down alongside me, and the driver rolled down his window. "I was just driving up here ten minutes ago," he said, "and there was a bear right next to the road." He pointed to a spot about a hundred or so yards away. "I thought you should know."

"Thanks," I said fervently. "I appreciate the tip." As he drove off, I started pedaling again, carefully scanning both sides of the road. Not glimpsing anything big and black, though, I had to wonder… was this second sighting another quirk of fate? But a day or so later, I had to swerve my bike around some bear scat in the middle of the road. I mean, it *had* to be from a bear. Nothing else but a really, *really* big animal could have produced such a large pile of uh, *stuff*.

You know the old saying. Once is a fluke, twice is a coincidence, but three times is a pattern. So it was official. Our neighborhood definitely had bears. No matter how beneficial home-grown compost would be, keeping a compost pile anywhere near our little farm would be "Bear Dumb."

62 🌿 Foothills Foodies

My dad spent his boyhood summers working in his grandmother's wheat fields, and my mom's father grew up on a farm. But when it comes to farming and country life, out of the two of us, John's the one with the street cred.

When I told Sue that I used to swim in the irrigation ditches on my grandpa's farm, she looked horrified. "They're filthy—you could have died!"

I learned later irrigation water is full of pesticides and animal waste and other harmful pollutants, but those swims didn't appear to hurt me any. In fact, our family's visits to Grandma and Grandpa Browne's farm in western Kansas were the best part of my summer vacations. After our dip, my brother and I would explore the barn, the orchard, and the cornfield. Grandpa and my father would take us out to the melon patch to sample watermelon and cantaloupe right off the vine. I can still remember how good that home-grown fruit tasted… you might say it was the start of my passion for gardening. After leaving the farm, we'd go see Grandma Dedie, on Mom's side, who raised chickens. From her I discovered where eggs came from.

But my own garden experiences actually started indoors, when I was about twelve, watching my mom peel potatoes. When she told me what the potato "eyes" were for, I asked if I could try growing some potatoes myself. I fixed up a garden patch, about two feet square, and after a few months, I was so excited to harvest my own little crop of 'taters. Even better was eating them!

By the time I had kids of my own, I had a modest-sized garden plot. One day, when my two kids were tots, they were "helping" me harvest rhubarb. Rhubarb leaves are poisonous, but I found one use for them. After cutting the stalks, instead of throwing away all the leaves, I saved a few of the biggest ones, and the three of us wore them as sunhats!

Even if farming runs in your blood, figuring out how to grow your own food has nothing to do with genes, and everything to do with learning by doing.

After abandoning my compost pile plans, I had to accept that our soil amendments would have to be trucked-in 'shroom compost or nothing. But there are some shortcuts through the garden school of hard knocks—like getting advice from your fellow Foothillies. My friend Lori told me that the growing season out here is a full month shorter than in town. A month! How could that be? We were only thirty-five miles away! Maybe her place, only a few miles away, was in one of those cold sinks, I told myself hopefully. In the lee of a big hill and surrounded by mature woods, her property could have a *completely* different climate than ours. But the summer nights I stepped outside to admire the stars reminded me of the oft-repeated Mark Twain joke. "The coldest winter I ever spent was the summer I was in San Francisco."

So after discovering that nighttime temps could be downright *cold*, John and I had to scramble to create veggie beds in whatever small pockets of heat and sun we had. I'd already used up a lot of prime veggie real estate with my perennial bed. What was left was some space next to the garage foundation. Time for more bed-building, which by now we had down to a science: pickaxing, rock and wood removal, spade-forking, then compost-spreading.

On this side of the yard, adjacent to the septic drain field, the rock population had to be four times that of my perennial bed. So with extra time out for rock management, not to mention backache breaks, within a couple of weeks, we had a few dozen square feet of arable earth. An awfully modest space for a farm, even a starter one, but enough to bulk up production of what we'd successfully grown back in town.

Off we went to the big box home and garden center in town. Although with my shopping allergy, most stores give me hives, I revel in plant-buying like a clotheshorse trolls for fashions at Bergdorf's. After living at Mom's the previous summer—and having to skip an entire gardening season—I joyfully filled our cart with zucchini squash, tomatoes, bell peppers, green bean starts, and herbs. In keeping with our veggie theme, John chose an outdoor thermometer with a friendly red tomato on the face.

As soon as we arrived home with our goodies, I took a closer look at the tags and scowled. "I don't believe this." I showed one to John. *Grown in Alabama.* I should have known a chain store would buy chain plants.

"But our climates aren't all that different," John commented, less bothered than I was (as he usually is) that we'd bought out-of-state nursery stock.

"You're probably right," I said, still torqued. But he had a point. Like a lot of places in the southern part of the U.S., Western Washington has mild winters, and our Mediterranean-like midsummers would give our plants a couple months of sunshine. Besides, our veggie "microclimate" next to the foundation would be as bright and hot for our plants as a tanning bed. John rigged up another Rube Goldberg fence, and as we settled our starts into their new home, I reminded myself we were old hands at growing zucchinis and tomatoes—we'd make these immigrant plants work.

We carefully composted, fertilized, and watered. But those southern belles from 'Bama only languished. Although in town, we'd raised a bumper crop of squash, peppers, and tomatoes in a few square feet of raised beds, this year's specimens just sort of *sat* there. I guess our chilly nights kept them too busy shivering to grow, because two weeks later, the zucchinis were the same size they'd been when we bought them. The hot peppers looked like they'd actually shrunk.

We were running out of time to grow much of anything. With mid-July upon us, I finally wised up and went plant-shopping again—to a real nursery this time—and came home with Northwest-grown tomato plants. We tucked them in the warmest spot in the yard, right next to the house foundation, and hoped for the best.

In spite of our setback, we did have a secret weapon for zucchini. Which is, if anyone can make them produce, it's John. Years ago, he introduced me to a naughty new garden pastime: zucchini sex. As we inspected our zuke patch, he'd pulled off a blossom, and showed me that fruiting veggies have male *and* female flowers. Who knew? And that they would actually have to make intimate contact—the female flower would have to have a male flower's pollen come a' callin', and touch her, um, you know. So if your resident bees aren't doing the job, it's up to you to wade through the zucchini hills and get those shy flowers to make whoopee.

And thus began a new Foothills morning routine. With the flowers freshly open, you'd find John knee-deep in the squash patch, tickling their fancies.

Now, all we needed was the weather to warm up.

63 🐝 The Weathergirl

Here in the Pacific Northwest, rain is mostly a lonely singleton: all you get is wet. But in the Midwest, things are different. Rain comes with thunderstorms, sort of like a co-dependent couple—one never goes anywhere without the other one tagging along.

As a little girl in Minnesota, I lived in terror of storms. From spring until fall, every dark cloud brought fear. Would we get thunder or lightning? Wind? All three? A nighttime tempest would find me cowering under the covers in my bed. For the worst storms, I'd climb into my sister's bed while she was sleeping and pull *her* covers over my head.

Thunderstorms also brought the potential for what really scared the bejeezus out of me: tornadoes. My siblings and I would watch *The Wizard of Oz* every time it came on TV, and though the cyclone scene made me sick with anxiety, I couldn't tear my eyes away. Long after the movie ended, all I could see was Dorothy being locked out of the storm cellar with the black, whirling funnel cloud practically on top of her. Upping the fright factor, my dad would tell stories about the tornadoes he'd experienced on his grandmother's Dakota farm. "They sound just like a freight train," he'd say in his understated way. "Peel off a barn roof like it's a bunch of cards."

One summer Saturday I noticed a greeny-yellow cast to the sky, with a boiling blackness at the horizon. Well, my dad hadn't watched barn roofs blow off for nothing. He collected my mom and us five kids, and ushered us down to the basement of our split level. My heart in my throat, the roar of wind filling my ears, I watched through the small basement windows as Dad's row of poplar trees in our yard bent horizontal. Happily, our house survived intact. But I must have sensed even then that knowledge was power…so off I went to pursue some.

If John is the source of All Fix-It Know-How, my dad was the Keeper of All-Around Knowledge. Ask him any question, on any topic—geography, history, astronomy, literature, music, you name it—he'd know something about it. But then, not every dad, even if he's a college professor, would read *The New York Times Almanac* for fun.

A couple weeks after the storm, I sought him out. Ever elusive, Dad wasn't in his study, but hoeing the family vegetable plot. My mom, who loves beautiful things, was in charge of the flower garden, while my dad, who didn't even like vegetables except for carrots, grew wax beans and corn. But no carrots. Go figure.

"What's that cloud, Daddy?" I asked, pointing to the big puffy cloud drifting by.

My dad leaned on his hoe. "Cumulus, I'd say."

I gestured to the feathery ones high overhead. "How about those?"

"Cirrus. They come with fair weather."

"What does that mean, 'fair?'"

"When there's blue sky."

I digested this. So, cirrus were the good clouds. "What about the clouds that make rain?"

"Nimbus." Dad went on to explain that nimbus were the gray kind, and when they combine with cumulus they pile up to create storms. I felt relieved. Now armed with the proper information, and able to identify oncoming thunderstorms, I could take cover before I got too scared to move.

My dad's cloud lecture proved to be useful. In our region, off-and-on showers are nature's specialty, particularly the misty rainfall folks call "liquid sunshine." Which means almost any cloud can have rain in it.

As a local weather-watcher since I moved to the West Coast in '75, I've learned to assess the clouds, trying to ferret out their secrets.

Around here, tornadoes are as scarce as yellow teeth in Tinseltown, but when you live in a rainy climate and cycle daily, you've got to stay on your weather toes. That is, before any bike ride you must ask yourself: are you going to get wet? You've got to figure out what direction the clouds are coming from, if they're dense enough to produce precip, and if they're going to bring significant rain, how soon.

I know what you're thinking: why don't I just check the weather on the Web? But with our slow Internet, it takes so long to bring up a site, I can practically get a ride and be home before the pages have loaded. Besides, when you embrace the slow and simple life, you can't get too dependent on technology. There is one downside though. Going with your intuition means you sometimes misjudge clouds and come home kind of wet. Or if you see an ominously dark cloud to the south, but tell yourself you can sneak in a quick ride before it lets loose, count on getting soaked to your underwear.

64 🌿 Nothin' But Blue Skies...

As gardeners, John and I have the usual love-hate relationship with rain: good for plants, yucky to work in. Gardening fans must also accept that what Mother Nature giveth, she also taketh away. We're talking precipitation.

Our region generally has chilly, showery Junes right up to the Fourth of July. Then the good times roll. We get gentle sunshine through July and August, broken by the occasional showers, and hardly a handful of eighty-degree days. With my thirty-plus years around Western Washington, I thought I'd seen it all. But one day in late June, John and I woke up to a hot, dry wind, so arid it chapped your lips and dried out the inside of your nose. By afternoon, in our shade-free yard, I felt like I'd stepped into Death Valley.

It was the summer Northeaster. And "hotter than Dutch love," as my dad would say in one of his rare politically incorrect moments. Just like in winter, this dry, relentless air mass sweeps down from the Canadian prairies and into the north part of our county. While this wind will bring fair skies, it's *loud*—sounds like a jet engine warming up for takeoff. As darkness fell that first hot day, I hoped the weather was a fluke. But as we got day after day of ninety-degree heat—and sometimes even near one-hundred—I realized this could be a regular thing.

You understand, we Western Washingtonians are hot-weather wussies, who hardly need air conditioners because we have moss growing between our toes. When it's ninety-two degrees in Georgia or Phoenix, folks are shivering and asking each other, "Whaddya think of this cold spell?" Out here at that temperature, with my Midwest heat tolerance long rinsed out of me, I feel like a chicken broiling over a spit.

Although John and I were tempted to stay in the house, lower the blinds, and settle down with some mint juleps, we had work to do. So we slathered on the sunscreen and stepped into the inferno.

John and I have an unfortunate gardening habit: we buy plants before we have any place to put them.

Just before the midsummer heat wave, we embarked on our biggest plant-shop ever to buy orchard stock. This would be a long-term investment—no chain store, southern-grown flora allowed—so we headed back to our Foothills nursery. After much consulting with one of their clerk-experts, John and I headed home with a pickup bed of locally grown fruit trees and cane berry crowns, and the biggest, most fruit-laden blueberry bushes the nursery carried. Although the blueberries were still weeks away from being edible, we could already taste those home-grown beauties.

As the scorching northeasterly winds rolled in, John started digging planting holes in the orchard. It was here, in the midday sun, that he truly honed his rock extraction skills. Through some quirk of fate, or because the rock gods liked a good laugh, there was always a giant stone right where he planned a tree or shrub, just as there'd been beneath each fencepost site. And with plants needing a much bigger hole than the posts, you had your work cut out for you.

You'd stick your shovel in the earth, hear an ominous scrape, and two hours later, sweating and swearing, you'd be hauling a two-foot diameter boulder out of the ground. It did no good to simply leave the rock where it was and pick another spot to dig. There would be another buried boulder, at least as big as the one you gave up on, waiting for you like a bogeyman.

With dozens of plants impatient for homes, I'd try my hand at pickaxing a hole here and there. But with our tomato thermometer registering 120 degrees (true, it wasn't nearly 120, but take the tomato out of direct sunlight and it was well past ninety), before long, I'd flee to the only shade around—my office. Battling fingers slipping on the keyboard, I felt guilty about John toiling in the hot sun, and knew I couldn't stay inside *all* the time. Because the weather had been good for one thing.

Our vegetables had finally started to grow.

Between the heat, the 'shroom compost, and John's whoopee, we were back in business. The zucchinis finally woke up from their summer nap, filling the beds and producing flowers like there was no next week. The first little fruits began to swell, then started putting on the inches. My Northwest-acclimated tomatoes next to the house were pumping out new growth until they were as tall as Mom's Mystery Plant.

While the broiling sun was just what the veggie doctor ordered, our orchard plantings, ensconced in the gravelly, fast-draining soil, were not happy. They wanted watering, and lots of it.

We knew these late July days were the worst time for planting, and this particular summer, we'd be doing it under the worst of conditions. But optimal planting time, say, mid-fall or early spring, seemed *years* away. John and I weren't willing to go slow—we wanted to build our orchard, grow our own food *now*.

In addition to often daily watering, consistent mulching for the orchard would be the order of the day. Though we still had a mountain of mushroom compost for top-dressing our plants, it was verboten for our thirsty new blueberries, raspberries, and cultivated blackberries. The nursery staff, wise in the Foothills ways, warned us that the compost was alkaline, when berries thrive in more acidic soils. "Too many salts," the clerk told us. For mulch, berries prefer composted steer manure. So John and I trekked back to the nursery for a locally made product, at six dollars for a couple of cubic feet, and bought three sacks of it.

As the sun dipped in the sky, I carefully parceled out a couple quarts of the rich, fluffy steer compost for each berry plant, smoothed it out to the drip line, and hoped our orchard offspring could hang in there until the fall rains came.

65 🦋 Livin' La Vida Local

Nowadays, you're often no more likely to know your neighbors than the folks you read about in *People* magazine. Maybe there's someone on your block you run into regularly, and they'll say, "Let's do coffee," but you never do.

I say, not in the boonies. Maybe no one's meeting over a cup of java, but people here, a bit like in the days of yore, do connect. Perhaps the love of the land creates some invisible bond between you. Or maybe it's all the other things you have in common, like not having cable or spending half your life in garden dirt or manure-encrusted jeans. Or that you're miles away from any social outlet, but still.

On my daily bike ride, my community outreach is pretty much exchanging waves with local drivers. While I'm home writing, though, John has revived the lost art of meeting the neighbors. He passes the time of day with the rancher living down at the main road, and on their occasional visits, the buyers of the property adjoining ours. He's also a regular at the organic mom-and-pop, and the clerks greet him by name. As a true Foothills insider, John has dropped the Hair Masters in town in favor of the village beautician. He'll sit in her oversized, old-fashioned leather barber's chair—it's more like a throne—while she dishes about who's related to whom, canning and preserving tips, and where you can buy farm-fresh anything.

After five months at our new place, which we figured was "miles from nowhere," John was getting as connected as a Hollywood talent agent.

Back at Berryridge, we had zucchini just about ready for picking. But after admiring the summer's food bounty in area fields, John and I were eager to add more goodies to our locally grown eating repertoire. At the same time, we were losing what little taste we had for the long trips to the city supermarket. The more we slowed down and settled into country life, the more uncomfortable we grew with food shopping so far from home.

Cut-rate prices are all very well, but I was so done with big-box stores anyway—especially since most of their inventory is imported from China. We heard China-produced food was starting to show up on supermarket shelves too. Then one July day, John returned from the Foothills nursery with a county Farm Guide booklet, and suddenly our low-tech light blinked on. Why buy packages spit out at a far-flung processing plant when you can purchase food—planted, grown and harvested by your "neighbors"—just miles away?

Outfitting our orchard with Foothills-grown trees and berries was just the beginning. A bit intoxicated with the notion of buying local food, John and I began taking expeditions around our part of the country, sussing out farms that had heretofore been just another barn or field we'd passed on our way to somewhere else.

On our country wanderings, we found a family veggie stand that sold tomatoes picked that day. Our first visit, no one was minding the place, but they'd put out a scale and a basket for the money. Imagine that—the honor system and old-fashioned trust, alive and well.

Around the corner we discovered a blueberry farm. Here, you can chat with the owners, a married couple who are also the pickers, the processors *and* who also have outside jobs. John and I came home with a ten-pound box of berries—unsprayed, the husband told us—for an embarrassingly low price. But the next visit, we picked our own—me, for the first time. Few summertime pleasures equal tying a five-gallon bucket around your waist and plucking berries off the bush until your fingers are stained blue and your back aches pleasantly from the weight, knowing that you'll have fresh-picked fruit for dessert.

A short drive away is a place that offers pasture-fed beef. Chatting with the proprietors is part of the fun there too. They escort you to their freezer so you can choose your own cuts, packaged right on the farm. That night, I fried up the hamburger we'd bought, and it even *smelled* more natural.

Buying local doesn't mean only food. Instead of using a commercial face cream, I patronize a county gal who sells homemade cream in small glass Mason jars. It's every bit as wholesome as the locally grown berries. When I go to her place for a new supply, she'll show me what's new in her garden, and we'll exchange planting tips. Buying cream, then, becomes a sideline—it's the connection that counts. Her product is made of olive oil and home-grown herbs, and it doesn't only soften your skin. It soothes bug bites, heals scrapes and skin irritations of all kinds, and even makes zits disappear! When it comes to drugstore skin products, I don't care if it's branded "all natural," because if you read the label, folks, most store-bought cream seems to be a chemical bath, formulated mostly of alcohol and acids. What do those compounds actually do to your Boomer skin, I ask you?

Whatever you're buying, spending an entire day hunting-and-gathering locally is part of the Slow Food, Slowed Down lifestyle. You could obtain similar items in a half hour in the grocery store, but buying your food, one-on-one with the farmer, is like riding Amtrak. It's the journey, not the destination.

Fifteen miles away from our place is a small town of a couple of thousand souls, if you count the farm families living around the perimeter. Before John and I moved, the town was simply another nondescript, homely little slowdown on some country road we'd traversed a few times. Now that we were county folks, the town had somehow transformed itself—became part of our community. So why not spend our money right here?

Like with food shopping, you can find cheaper prices in the city. But driving thirty-five miles to Lowe's, Rite-Aid, or the Ford place, when you can support the local building supply outfit, pharmacy, and auto repair shop, feels not only wasteful, but disloyal.

At any Starbuck's, I'm told, you've got your choice of 87,000 different beverages. In our little town, John visits a small coffee shop that offers a couple of dozen libations. Since too many choices, I've heard, plays havoc with your brain chemistry, here, you not only reduce that terrible dilemma of what to order, but avoid messing with your mind. Plus, the barista knows what you want to order before you do.

With all our landscaping chores, John and I were wearing out work gloves faster than an Indy 500 car burns through tires. And every task seemed to require a garden tool our current arsenal lacked. Quite fortuitously, we had not one, but two local sources for both—

the town's farm supply stores.

A tenderfoot when it comes to farm store shopping, upon stepping over the threshold of one of them, I was filled with wonder—not unlike my first visit as a wide-eyed five-year-old to Dayton's Christmas displays in Minneapolis. This particular farm store is kind of upscale—spiffy building, well-lit, the merchandise neatly arranged. Whether you need rabbit feed or electric fencing, it's easy to find. There's always a fresh-faced, if bored-looking young clerk behind the counter, so go to this store when you're short on time.

But if you're not, try the one in the slightly tatty pole building. It's as dark, dusty, and cobwebby as the haunted houses you see in movies, and the help is often invisible, more like a ghostly presence you sense in the back room. But you can buy neat items that you thought stores stopped selling a long time ago. We found a galvanized steel washtub that looks like it came straight out of the "Little House" books, with the idea of using it to store firewood. But in a pinch, you really could scrub a load of laundry in it. Or a toddler.

Espresso stands—often looking like miniature houses—are the new 7-11, sprouting on every city and suburban corner. In our little town, there's a dairy drive-through shaped like a small barn. You've got your choice of gallons, quarts, and even pints of milk, plus cream and butter—all from an area farm. The smiling clerk often has her toddler playing right next to her. By late afternoon, the after-work crowd is lining up.

It's the closest you'll ever get to a traffic jam. Unlike the city traffic we left, no one here seems to be in a hurry. You can actually drive the speed limit—twenty-five miles an hour—without someone riding your back bumper. Apparently the townsfolk agree that "slow" isn't just a speed, but a mindset.

Three or four miles from town there's a winery, where the vintners create wines and cordials from grapes and berries grown in their own fields. Go in any afternoon, and they'll give you a free taste of everything they make. The wines taste like summer—and after a few samples, you're already tipsy. But perhaps you came in that way, drunk on the beautiful farmlands-and-Foothills scenery.

You realize, of course, that I'm not going to tell you where this town is, or else you'd move here too. You and a lot of other people, that is.

Then Wal-Mart would feel obliged to pave over a dozen or so farms for a new store. Although anyone with a sensitive nose might not be tempted to settle here—the smell of manure sometimes overpowers the entire place. But if you can get past that, you're golden.

66 ❦ Berryridge Banditos

In a lot of Westerns, there's a payload-laden train crossing vast, empty stretches of territory that invariably attracts desperados like flies to fresh buffalo chips. If you ask me, sending out a lone rider here and there with the cash in their saddlebags would have been smarter, because nobody, especially robbers, would pay attention to them. (But then you wouldn't have much of a movie.)

Our thriving, late summer garden was like that Wild West train full of money—now, we had more loot to defend. While deer were already our sworn garden foe, a new kind of bandit descended upon us: Public Enemy #2.

I'd always thought of rabbits as gentle, pretty creatures (you know, like deer). I'd loved the greeting cards my sister gave me featuring sweet little bunny families, and admired the peaceful animals you see in the Rabbit House at the county fair.

Don't kid yourself. What the deer don't finish off, the rabbits will. And while deer will give a plant an unsightly haircut, the rabbits will barber one down to a bald pate. They ate half of my treasured heavenly bamboo shrub, while a cranberry plant, high country huckleberry, sea pinks, lilies, and asparagus tips all got buzzed to the ground.

And it's even harder to rabbit-proof your plantings than deer-proof. I thought my eyes had deceived me when I saw a rabbit slip through two-inch poultry fencing without a break in its stride, but we had the proof seeing new blueberry shoots neatly nipped to the soil line. "I wish the coyotes or bobcats or whatever else is around here would get on the job," I said, exasperated.

"There's always rabbit stew," John growled.

But he resisted his inner Elmer Fudd, probably because the rabbits left our main produce unmolested. Thus each night, we had fresh-picked zucchinis, stir-fried, roasted, or if we're in a hurry, microwaved with a dab of butter. With the heat ripening our dozens of tomatoes, we also feasted on tomato sandwiches, tomato salad, or John's no-fuss favorite, sliced with a dash of salt and pepper. Already smacking our lips over our ripening blueberries, we entered the orchard a few days later for another inspection.

But the berries had disappeared. Robins, those cheery harbingers of spring, had pillaged our small crop as ruthlessly as the Goths sacked ancient Rome. Before we thought to net our bushes, they'd nabbed every last blueberry, even the white ones. "Next year," I said darkly, "these suckers'll be sorry. I'm netting in May."

We have yet another resident robber, one that strikes terror in the heart of woman, especially a Dirty Single-Wide Survivor. It's the one you never see much of, but whose presence is easily detected.

The Country Mouse. And I don't mean the dowdy kind.

As you downsizers know, moving into a smaller home doesn't exactly mean you've instantly simplified your life. No matter how well you think you've "edited" your possessions, you're somehow still left with acres of boxes you've got no room for. John and I were done throwing all that money at storage units, and we had a little extra room in the shop because of our scrapped plans for John's office. So it naturally turned into our all-around storage site.

Of course, we knew we had mice around. We'd seen their nests outside, near our woodpiles—funny little clutches of seeds, leaf bits, and cottonwood fluff. Kinda cute, really. Then one August afternoon, embarking on one of our periodic, desultory unpacking sessions, John and I discovered the shop had acquired some new items. Mouse droppings. On the floor, on boxes, all over the outdoor grill I'd meticulously cleaned before we moved. Even sprinkled all over the top of the garbage bin. Wrinkling my nose in disgust, I wondered aloud, "How do you think they climbed up that smooth plastic?"

"They just find a way," John said grimly. Unearthing yet another poo-covered box, he made a face.

I located my industrial-strength rubber gloves I kept for really dirty jobs, and gingerly unpacked around the droppings. "At least they can't get at stuff we really care about," I said. Like the winter clothes stored in thick construction-grade garbage sacks, sealed with oodles of tape.

Hauling one of them out to unpack John's flannel shirts and jammies for washing, I found the clothing rife with holes. "Gross!" I dragged the sack into the driveway, and lifted each garment out with a glove-encased thumb and forefinger. Some holes were small, but two pairs of John's favorite pajama bottoms were completely ruined. All accomplished with apparently no entryway. Or exit either. Still, there was certainly no mouse in the sack.

Not long after, I decided it was way past time to check the oil in my car. I lifted the hood, and sitting on top of the car engine was a mouse nest the size of a man's hand. My big question: how could they have built such a substantial home in the couple of days since the car had last been driven?

Or, unbeknownst to me, had they been doing a long-term mouse ride-along with me, like a police officer in training? That's one Berryridge mystery, I fear, that will never be solved. But that we had a Big Mouse Problem there could be no doubt. Off John went to stock up on mousetraps, and thus began the mouse hunter's equivalent of D-Day. Just as the Allies took France back from the Germans, John initiated a ground assault to reclaim the garage from the mice.

He learned from the nursery folks that orchard mouse populations are truly mind-boggling: up to a *million* per acre. Hard to control those numbers with a few traps. Thus, our War on Mice would be more of an ongoing campaign, rather than a Mission Accomplished. At least we didn't have to worry about mouse-proofing the inside of our house. Between the crawlspace and the floor, a manufactured home is sealed with thick, impermeable plastic—a "belly," it's called—so your entire dwelling is shrink-wrapped, as pest-secure as a steel box. Whatever happened, we were well protected.

Or we were, until the day I opened the bathroom cupboard. Underneath the wastepaper basket, I discovered those dark, unmistakable bits that could only mean... I slammed the cupboard shut. "John!" I hollered. "We have mice! In the *house*!"

In a past life, I was known as The Terminator.

Actually, it was a well-kept secret, from way back when I collected pollywogs in my tee-shirt. When I got home, I put them in a large can of water—I wanted to see them lose their tails and become frogs. I suppose I was like a lot of boys (you know, big on "snakes and snails and puppy-dogs' tails"), because I had an element of not just curiosity, but cruelty. For some reason, lost on me now, I started mashing these frogs with a stone. I don't remember how many I had killed before my Grandma Grace caught me, looking aghast. "How would you like it if you were in their place?" she asked. I felt immediately ashamed and set the rest of the frogs free.

Grandma never told anyone else about it—and it was the first and last time I killed living things for sport. After I became a gardener, I was especially appalled at what I'd done, since I discovered frogs and toads make a banquet of garden pests and mosquitoes. So, these days, I try to respect living things. At our new place, I run what Sue calls, "John's Insect Escort Service." Bugs in the house get "taken out"—not as in exterminated, but as in, ushered outside. We figure that having a naturally healthy garden means a live-and-let-live attitude toward bugs of all kinds.

I have some exceptions to my "respect" mindset, though. Hornets' nests get knocked out, slugs are dispatched upon sighting, and one huge spider we found in the house, that we suspected was a Black Widow, got squished. So do indoor ants, but we're working on an all-natural ant repellent. To mice, however, I show no mercy. Give me a trap and a spoon of peanut butter, and I'll show you...well, never mind.

67 🦋 It's Not Easy Being Green

When I was sixteen, my dad pulled into the driveway with a '71 scarlet-red Ford Cougar.

Spanking-new, this car's flamboyance, its utter *hotness* was worlds away from our family's sensible station wagons. With a V-8 engine powering its modestly-sized chassis, The Coug, when idled, shimmied like Elvis. On the freeway, one tap on the accelerator could take that sleek little cat to eighty-five mph. I loved that car.

But it was the last V-8 I'd ever drive. Small cars—practically *de rigueur* for an environmental studies major—would be my future, even if my heart would forever belong to that gas-hogging speedster. Of course, you don't need to be a rabid environmentalist to pursue the other basics of sustainability—like eschewing mouse poison, recycling, and not buying more than one house made almost entirely of plastic.

Now that we were going for the simple life, I redoubled my efforts toward sustainable living. Minimal trips to town and minimal waste. (In spite of our garbage-bound, instead of compost-bound, kitchen scraps.) I liked the idea of working our acreage by hand instead of using a tractor, and not increasing greenhouse gases, even if John's fondest dream is buying a little green John Deere. But I didn't really want a tractor anyway. Besides the noise and smell, we'd have missed out on all that fun with the pickax.

True, we'd been lavish with garden watering through July and August, but John and I had a low-water use front-load washer, water-saving showerheads, and we'd quit washing our cars. (I admit we didn't give up car-washing to save water, though. Once you live on a gravel road, that in wet weather covers your car with mud, and dry weather coats it with dust, there's just no point.) Even though Garrett, our environmentally friendly contractor, had said we'd have an inexhaustible supply of water from our well, for our efforts to save, the gods of conservation would surely smile upon us.

Maybe they could make up for our decidedly non-greenie, albeit low-emissions heating source. "The woodstove might not be all *that* bad for the environment," I said soon after we'd had it installed. "Probably not any more polluting than a propane furnace."

"Especially when you figure in the gasoline for delivering the propane," John agreed.

"I hear fallen trees create greenhouse gases in their decomposition process anyway," I added virtuously.

Besides, think of all that hot air that gets emitted into the atmosphere when you're hyperventilating over your propane bill. So heating with a woodstove could actually be a lot more environmental than it got credit for.

All summer, the stove had sat unused in the corner—black, boxy, and homely as a hound. But as we drifted into mid-September, the nights growing not just cooler, but often cold, our stove started looking far more attractive. As the time to fire it up grew closer, John got to thinking about our firewood supply, and not one to sit on his hands, he hustled to saw up our collection of birch boughs. But somehow, as the chill mornings warmed into seventy-five degrees by noon, it was hard to think about firewood.

Instead, fall garden chores demanded center stage.

You know summer's winding down when your zucchinis start turning lime-green.

The leaves turn gray with powdery mildew, and so do your pea vines. Your pole beans look sort of shrively, and the pickins' are sparse. The season's raspberry canes are withering and need to be cut out, the new ones tied up for winter. With the hot summer, Berryridge Farm had attracted great tomato karma—most had vine-ripened, and were relatively blight-free. The first frost, though, would hit any day now—time to pick the last tomato stragglers, to hopefully ripen in the garage. And since there's nothing more depressing than a garden full of black plant corpses, we pulled up the remains of the vegetables and covered the empty beds with mushroom compost.

But the rest of the place was a weed-and-wood dump.

Garrett had lightened our carbon footprint considerably by refusing, in his sweet way, to burn the slash mountain in front of our living room. By the summer's end, however, I was ready to give his weenie roast idea a go.

The modest brush piles he'd left in the yard had grown to the size of Volkswagen Beetles. For months, I'd collected wheelbarrow loads of sticks and limbs to throw on the mounds, and as they expanded, I'd stared balefully at the mess—it was like household clutter you're forbidden to throw out. Add the wood, some rotten, some not, that John and I had mined from our garden beds, plus the six-foot tall fireweed and bracken fern we'd bushwhacked, and we had more yard waste than we knew what to do with.

Even a Greenie has her limits. There was nothing else to do but burn it.

You understand that despite our region's nine or ten months of wet weather, you can't burn just any old time. Little rain falls in July and August, and often well into September. And given the plentitude of forestlands, outdoor burning is a no-no, whether it's waste from logging operations or a backyard bonfire. During this particular summer, with the hottest, driest conditions most people around here could remember, burning would be not only legally verboten, but stupid—especially in outlying areas like ours, with fire stations few and far between. Generally speaking, then, you're not permitted to light so much as a twig in your yard from early summer to mid-fall.

I was so done looking at those gigantic brush heaps loitering in our yard—yet the burn ban was still in play. The temptation to cheat was always there, but John, a by-the-book kind of guy, as well as a former cop, feels especially honor bound to stay on the right side of the law. So we held our fire.

That is, until early October. When the burn ban was lifted, I was as eager to light up as a nicotine-deprived smoker with a ciggie.

68 ❧ October Surprise

One of the great pleasures of being a kid is playing outside and not giving a rip how dirty you get. For our Big Burn, I put on my grubbiest gardening clothes, prepared to be at one with smoke and soot. I'd always been the kind of careful child who didn't like getting grimy, so my newly discovered embrace-your-dirt approach was as freeing as a skinny dip.

We followed Garrett's suggestion and set aside a whole day for burning. It was a hot day for October, and all our weeds and wood scraps, well-seasoned by the dry summer, would be prime tinder. Once I brought out a book of matches and some newspaper, we selected a burn site in the middle of the yard, and John got a decent little bonfire up and running in no time.

Since he was the head fire marshal, I was the fire feeder. I'd drag boughs and small stumps and crackly-brown fireweed carcasses into the fire, then it was back to the brush mounds or berm for another load. While my housewifely soul rejoiced at finally tidying up our messy yard, my clothes and bare arms and legs grew filthier and filthier.

The burning went on into evening, but as dusk approached, we still had lots of wood junk that hadn't made it to the burn pile. Hungry and exhausted, John and I took stock of the waning light and figured we'd live to burn another day. While he got out the hose, I took a quick walk to stretch my stiff back.

When I returned, he'd just finished drowning our burn site. Always cautious, John wouldn't leave even the tiniest of embers to threaten the still-dry woods around us. I went inside to peel off my sooty clothes, craving a shower far more than food. I turned on the tap and oddly, only a small stream emerged. I turned up the pressure, but got the merest trickle. Then…nothing.

We were out of water.

69 ❦ Waterworld

Garrett, our Yoda, had been wrong. Wronger than wrong. The endless runoff from the ring of hills surrounding us, which was *supposed* to fill the aquifer we were sitting on, clearly had not. Maybe the aquifer had, well…shrunk.

Or else I'd completely depleted it with my berry-watering.

John called Garrett straight off. Garrett couldn't diagnose the problem over the phone, but he did advise John to flip off the well pump breaker. That way, your expensive pump won't grind away, sucking air instead of water and overheating, thereby melting the wiring and plastic casing. That night, we had no choice but to climb into bed unshowered and reeking of smoke. First thing in the morning, we phoned the well-drilling folks as Garrett suggested, but they couldn't come out until the following day. As everyone knows, you never quite appreciate something until it's gone. And let me tell you, in a few short hours we developed an acute, everlasting gratitude for running water.

The drilling folks showed up as promised, and made their measurements. The paperwork for our well, drilled two years before, had indicated a forty-foot column of water. But as of today, that plentiful column had dwindled to less than four feet—the water level had dropped to just beneath the pump. Their temporary fix was to lower the pump into the short column of remaining water, one foot from the bottom of the well.

The permanent solution was to drill deeper.

Well, you gotta have water—so John and I couldn't worry about the cost of sinking the well deeper. But we could about the timing. Because at the moment, we had one scant foot of water...and the well folks wouldn't be able to come out to drill for another two weeks.

If we'd had a long two days without water, the next two weeks dragged. We became the poster kids for water conservation. Navy showers. Few dishes washed. And no laundry.

Drill Day arrived, and along with it, one of our Pacific Northwest monsoons, fondly nicknamed the "Pineapple Express." These are warm fall rains, fed from a seemingly endless offshore flow from Hawaii. No liquid sunshine here; the downpour soaked the earth, with no sign of letting up. The well-drillers called, and said they couldn't drill in such wet conditions. Weather permitting, they'd try for the next day. So—another twenty-four anxious hours. Would our water hold out? Or would we experience the extreme irony of running out of it on one of the rainiest days on record?

The next morning dawned with clear blue skies—and we still had water. But not a moment too soon (at least for me), out came the well people with their Brontosaurus-sized drilling rig.

While I worked inside, John hung out next to the rig, and got a crash course in well-drilling. The driller guys figured the well would be as good as new if they went down twenty feet. After a half-day of drilling, however, they hit a layer of clay. Not gonna work. They had to drill another twenty, to a more water-supply friendly substrate layer, making forty feet in all.

Two days later, the mail brought an eye-popping drill-bill: $3200. We already knew the Foothills life was going to cost us. And now, we had yet another budget-busting invoice sitting in our stack of bills. But we were back in business…water!

You can say that again.

That sunny day turned out to be the last gasp of Indian summer. As if to compensate for the dry July, August, and September—not to mention our dry well—system after system rolled in, drenching not only the Foothills but the entire region. Rivers flowed over their banks. Basements flooded. Mudslides slid. In town, we would have viewed all this rain as annoying, even depressing. But now, after our well troubles, each rainstorm was something to be grateful for—it would help replenish the aquifer.

Soon after the well-drilling, John stood at the kitchen window and surveyed our firewood supply, stacked out of the rain—sort of—against the shop. "We've got to get a shed up," he announced. Since John collects lumber like Star Trekkers collect action figures, I assumed we'd have plenty of building supplies on hand. As it turns out, except for some metal roofing left over from the shop construction, we pretty much needed to buy all new: treated 4 x 4s for the posts, 2 x 4s for the frame, plus siding. After the outlay for the well-drilling, thrilled I was not with another hit to the charge card. But like John, I wanted a proper woodshed, not a bunch of little storage huts squatting all over our property. And like the woodstove, the woodshed wasn't an expense, it was an *investment*.

John and I cleared a big section of brush just outside our yard, next to the shop, clipping bracken fern, tearing out birch saplings, and digging up knotty-rooted thimbleberry. Soon he'd constructed a stout shelter that would hold close to two cords, angled just right to avoid the driving late fall and winter rains.

John and I ferried our stack of birch logs inside, to find it barely filled one corner of the shed. In an amazing stroke of luck, though, a couple of days later we found a huge alder lying next to the entry of our private road. John's face lit up. "Alder's the best firewood there is."

We'd had no wind to speak of—my guess is the ground had become so saturated that the tree's roots lost purchase in the soil. Before another firewood scarfer could beat him to it, John changed into his workduds and jumped into the pickup to salvage some of the downed tree. Actually, "savage" is a better descriptor—John wrestled with these logs for hours, hand-sawing and chain-sawing and just plain hacking the green wood into more manageable chunks. I helped him lever the logs upright so he could heft them into the truck—which levered his back out of alignment. But hey, it was more free firewood!

Happily, we had some cedar and maple rounds we'd gotten from a neighbor back in town for the coming winter. Now, John became single-minded about filling the shed. Shrugging on his raincoat, he'd sit in the middle of the yard, a cedar piece for his stool, and doggedly split rounds and cut still more birch. As the hours passed, rain would drip off his ballcap, while the ruts surrounding him grew from puddles into ponds. He came in from the rain one day and said, "I think we need a cutting shed."

I was all for it—I'd felt plenty guilty working indoors while my steadfast wood-wrassler was stuck out in the weather. After we cleared more ground next to the new woodshed, John once again hit the local building supply store. I was already sure life here would be more expensive than in town. But as I helped John unload the lumber and roofing, it struck me forcibly that Berryridge Farm would actually be much more of a money-sucking enterprise than we could have ever imagined. With the well-drilling bill, and now hundreds more spent on building supplies, our Visa balance was starting to feel like the operating budget for a mid-sized city.

Once the cutting shed was up, John got back to wood processing. But for all his labors, his "fruit" added up to maybe a third of a cord of firewood. The good news was, we wouldn't see much cold weather until after the New Year. Which gave us well over two months to work on our wood supply.

70 ❧ Playing with Matches

You've heard the joke. "It takes one careless match to light a forest fire. But it takes a whole box of them to light a campfire."

Or a woodstove. When getting out of bed in the mornings became almost painful, John and I decided that it was time for our stove's baptism by fire. It was then we learned that heating with wood is all about "teachable moments."

I thought building a fire in our stove would be a snap. After all, I was an old hand with campfires and fireplace fires. So for my debut woodstove fire, I laid out my wood in my usual campfire set-up, and applied a match. But instead of the smoke going up the stovepipe, it rolled out the front of the stove and into my face. I discovered one good thing though—our smoke detectors were in fine working order.

We had several more smoke-outs, so bad that Sue and I had to open every window in the house. (Which meant several hours of wood burning to get our house to the temperature it was before I started.) Frustrated, Sue got out the woodstove operating manual. "It says here you're supposed to heat the flue first by burning some newspaper."

"I guess we missed that part," I said ruefully. Though I'd dropped a peg or two on the credibility meter, I started over, burning two sheets of newspaper in the firebox. (I learned a lot depends on what kind of newsprint you use. The heavier-grade paper used by Sue's fluffo newspaper smokes more than the lighter-weight kind of *The Seattle Times* or *P-I.*)

Sure enough, pre-heating the flue did the trick—except when it didn't.

I started lots of fires where I could feel cold air rush down the stovepipe into the firebox. The newspaper wouldn't light properly, only smolder—and though I'd quickly close the stove door, smoke would still leak out. For a long time, I thought some wonky barometric air pressure was creating a downdraft. Then I discovered why smoke was being drawn into the room instead of up the pipe: house exhaust fans. So before you so much as strike your first match, whether to preheat your flue or light your fire, make sure you've got all your fans—main ventilation fan, bathroom fans, or the one over the range—in the "Off" position.

After trying lots of wood configurations, I've found a system that consistently works. First, I do the flue-warming step. Then I set two smallish pieces of wood parallel in the firebox, then lay kindling (four to eight-inches long, one-half to one inch in diameter) in a crosshatch pattern. Next, I slip a small log or split piece of wood in the cavity beneath the kindling, then another one on top, across the two parallel pieces. Using six to eight-inch square pieces of newspaper, I crumple one up and tuck it in the cavity, then, one at a time, light more squares of newspaper and stuff them under the kindling until both the kindling, the piece of wood in the cavity and the top one catch fire. Once they're going, I add a couple of larger chunks of firewood in a teepee pattern and shut the door. After about ten minutes, when everything is burning steadily, I put a good-sized piece of wood on top. All I have to do is add another log or two every half hour.

Building a woodstove fire is as much an art as a science, if I do say so myself. Once you master the basics—how to adjust for the size and dryness of your kindling and fuel, your air flow, and all the other variables—you're pretty much home free.

The one disappointment to heating with wood (once John and I got past the smoke-outs) was discovering just many birch logs it took to heat our house for a mere evening. But within a day or two, I realized what our new heat source was *really* all about: Dirt. I'd already discovered country housekeeping is more intensive than in the city. But using a woodstove requires a whole new level. If you like a clean house, do not, I repeat, DO NOT install a woodstove.

Firewood comes from nature—so naturally, it has particles of soil, dust, and lichen clinging to it. And when you bring your wood into the house, all those bits, plus various bark and wood fragments, invariably get sprinkled onto your floors and carpet, especially around your stove. Once the woodstove is operating, you're counting on that simulated tile floor mat you spent several hundred dollars on to protect the area immediately surrounding it. But no—your woodstove scoffs at such paltry attempts to confine the mess. Feeding the fire one day, I watched, aghast, as a big ol' cinder flew out of the stove and left a black scar on the carpet three feet away. If I'd only known how far a stove could spew ash and soot, I'd have installed a mat three times the size of the one we bought.

Note to woodstove retailers: This is where you folks have made a grave error, not having a dirt-aware salesperson on staff. Really, you could be generating tons more profit, selling much, *much* bigger floor mats. The sales guy never told me the one we'd bought was way too small, but then, maybe he's like a lot of other folks (and sorry, guys, they're mostly men)—he just doesn't *see* dirt. I'm not talking figuratively—I think some people have a kind of vision anomaly that prevents dirt from registering on their retinas.

I have often pondered how much more free time I'd have if only I could develop that ability too. Because soot presents never-before-seen cleaning challenges. There's a greasy feel to it, not unlike used motor oil. And once the soot hits your carpet, it's there to stay, impervious to soap and water. You can try spot-cleaning that big black smudge on your carpet, but what you'll end up with is a much bigger gray one. And if you've got new carpeting? I swear it crooks its finger at the stove, and with an inviting glance says, "Come on, honey, give me that lived-in look."

It's the same with your attire. No matter how careful you are, if you're tending the stove, you'll find black streaks on your sleeves and pants, as well as other odd places, like behind your knee, that you swear could never have touched the stove. Sometimes it just doesn't pay to wear clean clothes.

And a lot of days, it doesn't pay to clean the house. The furniture near the stove will sport an ash layer within hours of dusting. And even the supposedly small amount of emissions that escape an airtight, EPA-approved stove leaves a film on your windows, so on a sunny day, they resemble tinted glass. With only greenish firewood to burn, John and I figured we had no choice but to bring some into the gravel room for further seasoning. Which meant more splinters and bark bits and lichen making their way into the main part of the house.

But with nighttime temps often dipping below forty, I admit the woodstove, for all its faults, grew on me. Especially one particular Sunday morning.

I woke up early, to an odd sound—a low, whooshing kind of whine. Our hard-working rancher neighbor must have fired up his tractor, I thought sleepily. As John rose for the day, I pulled the covers over my head for a nice weekend lie-in, and fell back to sleep.

When I next awakened, the bedroom felt unusually chilly. And the steady, whiny drone was still there. Man, for a Sunday, he's going hard at it, I thought. Then I parted the blinds and peered outside to find a stiff wind blowing, the trees curved toward the south. A Northeaster? On October twenty-seventh?

Back in town, Northeasters were more of a January thing. Apparently, winters might start a little earlier out here. I dressed quickly, and headed for our sure-to-be warm living room and found John putting another log on the fire. "What do you think of this? A Northeaster, for Pete sakes!"

John shrugged philosophically. "The stove'll keep us warm."

Overnight, the cold, dry wind had turned the scarlet leaves of our young sweet gum tree brown and withered, and the remnants of our summer perennials looked downright desiccated. As I wrapped my chilly hands around a hot mug of tea, I gave thanks for our woodstove. Sure, our wood-heating project had cost thousands. And if time was money, John and I were spending a *lot* of cashola on splitting and cleaning.

But hey. You can't put a price on comfort.

71 ❧ Crazy November

November in the Pacific Northwest is notorious for changeable weather. We get it all—rain, sleet, frost, and wind. Sometimes all at the same time. Any longtime resident will remember the infamous Thanksgiving Day Windstorm, back in the eighties, when power went out all over the region. To this day, people still tell stories about how they cooked their holiday turkey in their outdoor barbeque.

To add insult to infamy, November is *dark*. Once Standard Time takes effect, the daylight hours seem to go faster than the blink of your sunshine-starved eyes. If it's raining, it feels like you missed the daylight altogether. And when you lack next-door neighbors, there are no porch lights nearby to alleviate the darkness.

But for gardeners, there's a platinum lining to those November clouds—if you don't mind being lashed by rain, that is. It's a great time to plant. In a celebratory mood after our well was up and running again, and dreaming of expanding our little farm, John and I treated ourselves to another visit to the Foothills nursery. Of course, this time of year, vegetable-growing was out. Instead, we splurged on a hundred bucks' worth of "dress-up" plants—a California lilac, a couple of pistemons, a Bay shrub, Strawberry tree, and a lovely tall Himalayan honeysuckle I could picture in front of our dining room window.

Too bad we had no Berryridge Fairy Godmother around, waving her magic wand to instantly create planting beds. The paradox of November gardening is that although it's a prime opportunity to get plants in the ground, the soil is too wet to be worked. Thus, with pickaxing denied us, John and I parked our baby shrubs on the north side of the shop, under the eaves. Last year, our little plant refugees had wintered over in their pots without any cosseting—the new kids would be fine for a few weeks until we could give them a permanent home.

To be truthful, I was ready for a break from sod-busting—I'd spent the better part of seven months battling the elements, not to mention various intruders. So with rainy, dark, un-plantable November upon us, and a big project sitting on my desk, I was ready to put my nose to the professional grindstone. Committing to a tight deadline, I planted myself in front of my laptop, and hit the keys running.

I told myself I didn't mind the prospect of spending the next few weeks pretty well indoors, but after the months of joyful gardening, I found myself envying John and his wood-gathering chores (even if the weather wasn't the greatest). But at least I'd have my usual bike-ride breather each afternoon. I was exactly halfway through my project when November fifteenth dawned…

A day that brought a whole new element to the Foothills' earth, water, and fire.

72 🦋 Weathergirl on Alert

It began like any other November day—wet—though a stiff breeze had come up. Unfazed, I climbed on my bike and headed out. In town, riding in your basic November zephyr would often mean getting blown all over the road. At times, you'd have to stand up and pedal, and it would still feel like you were traveling backwards. So a little wind wasn't about to stop me.

Out I went, riding southwest on the main road. The wind seemed to be picking up with each revolution of my wheels, but since the rain had eased up, I kept going.

The main road here is lined by fir trees—big cedars and Douglas firs, many decades old, most fifty to eighty feet high, as well as smaller hemlocks, maybe thirty to forty feet in height. I always looked at these tall trees fondly as I rode by, appreciating the way they protected me from the elements. In hot weather, you get shade; in wet, the boughs overhead keep you from getting soaked. And on breezy days, the canopy acts as a windbreak. High above, conditions can be blustery, but at road level, the tree branches are hardly stirring. You feel quite sheltered—maybe even a bit like Pippin and Merry in "Lord of the Rings," where our little Hobbits are carried in the protective arms of Treebeard, one of the giant Ents.

But today felt…different. The trees began swaying in an ominous dance new to me. In town, on windy days like this, I'd ride on roads that were, naturally, bordered by houses and commercial establishments and genteel, well-pruned city trees. Not like out here, with huge trees, old trees, and even ancient, rotting trees. Or trees a lot like the giant alder next to our drive that had keeled over without provocation a month ago. And today, there was plenty of home-grown windpower to help more trees on their way down.

After riding for three-quarters of an hour, I was getting not only nervous, but scared.

I turned around just as the wind intensity seemed to leap. I'd gone a mile when I encountered a tree lying across the road—which had occurred in the fifteen minutes since I'd passed this spot. Dismounting, I had to push my bike through the roadside ditch to get around the fallen tree. And I still had five miles to go.

As I cycled eastward, the trees swirled madly above me. They seemed sinister now. All I could hear was the roar of the wind through the firs, the crack of boughs breaking. All I saw were chunks and branches raining down around me. And the closer I got to home, the more fallen trees I saw.

Terror coiled in my stomach. Going out in this storm had been worse than foolhardy. Worse than stupid. It was insane. My mother's best friend had lost her husband during a windstorm, when he'd gone outside and a tree had fallen on him. Would I meet the same fate? I pedaled furiously, my legs aching, my lungs burning. All I could think was, *I've got to get home.*

It was the longest, most nerve-wracking five miles I'd ever ridden. I turned into our private road, safe at last from the threat of falling trees. And I knew, more than any other time in my adult life, that there really is no place like home. With trembling legs, I managed the last mile, and met John at the kitchen door. "The power went out about twenty minutes ago," he said. "We're supposed to have a big windstorm."

"I think it's already here," I said shakily, and told him about the fright I'd just had.

"But you made it," my ever-practical John said, patting my shoulder, then he hurried outside to put away the stray pots and garden tools in the yard. Safely inside, I looked out at our sapling-covered acres, thankful we had no tall firs close enough to endanger the house.

So. No power. Which meant our water supply would be limited to what we had in the pumphouse tank. We had no operational phone either, so I couldn't even call the power company about the outage. But there were sure to be other folks in the area—folks with cell phones—without power too. The one thing we did have was warmth…our woodstove.

While we still had some water pressure, I got busy filling pots and pitchers for drinking and cooking. As the winds raged around Berryridge, though, our plain vanilla house didn't even rattle—it was as solid as I'd suspected the first time I'd walked in. As John came back inside, I said, "Did you notice? The house is like, not shaking."

"Garrett did a great job," John said, smiling, and fetched a book to while away the afternoon. Or maybe, I thought whimsically, the house had put down the same kind of roots in Berryridge land that John and I had.

Now that I'd recovered from my scare, it was back to the computer. Funny, how fast your creativity goes downhill when you're worried about your battery going dead. But surely the outage wouldn't last long. The ones we'd had in town had been short, maybe an hour or so. The longest outage hadn't even been storm-related, but some driver crashing into a power pole.

As the afternoon waned, so did the light, and by 4:30, it was too dark to do much of anything. With a sigh, John set his book aside and got out his big flashlight. By now, the wind had diminished a little, so ever optimistic, I said, "We'll probably have power by dinnertime."

We did not. Interesting, how hunger makes you more inventive. It's probably how early man figured out how to make fire, because he was sick and tired of raw mastodon steak. That night, inspired by Old Style Camping, John got us on board with a new skill—woodstove cooking. We fashioned some decent chow by heating leftovers in a pan on the top of the woodstove, and some veggies in foil alongside the pan. John also tucked two foil-wrapped potatoes next to the coals. Since the potatoes took almost an hour and a half, the meal was Slow Food at its most basic.

The mystics believe that out of the darkness comes illumination. All I learned was that dinner by candlelight isn't the least bit romantic when you don't have any choice. Once we were finished, I lit three more candles at the dining room table so I could write longhand, but by now, I had bigger worries than staying on top of my work schedule. After ten hours without power, our running water was down to a trickle.

73 ❧ Power to the People

There's a reason electricity is called power. Without it, you feel powerless.

And humbled. Although you get a new appreciation for modern conveniences, you've also got the challenge of keeping romance alive when your hair is dirty and you have to share toilet flushes. Even for germ-watchers, it's washing your fingertips or nothing. Too, when you can't work or do any other computer activity, use the phone, watch a movie, do housework or laundry, or take a shower, time slows to a crawl. Actually, it seems to stop. You feel you have no past, no future. Only the present. A present that involves a quickly dwindling water supply.

This is where John's credo comes in handy, about being okay with "what is." And a power outage is the ideal time to put not only Slow Food, but Slow Everything into practice. The next morning, John and I roused to a dark, silent house—on our own time, without an alarm clock to jolt us awake—to find the wind had subsided. Making tea for breakfast, I learned a watched pot, when it's on top of the woodstove, takes *forever* to boil.

Now that it was safe to be out on the roads, John headed to the village to buy bottled water. I climbed back on my bike for a look around myself, and on the main road, discovered an eerie landscape. Goggle-eyed, I maneuvered around branches, limbs, and entire trees lying in the roadway, or on the side of the road. More trees hung on power lines. Snapped electrical cables dangled from power poles, others lay right on the road. On the half-bald top of a nearby hill, a stand of firs left after a logging operation was flattened sideways, like a bad comb-over. If I needed an extra lesson about why you shouldn't ride your bike in a Foothills windstorm, this was it.

John came home with two five-gallon jugs of precious water—enough to flush each toilet! After my burst of elation, though, the second day without electricity dragged on.

Forced into a no-power, slower rhythm of life, you feel like you have all the time in the world. Sitting in the shadowy candlelight with your mate, with nothing to occupy you—something you're otherwise too busy for—you might do a little childhood reminiscing...or even chat about deeper, more personal subjects. Still, you can't help staring at the lights, missing the constant *whisht* of the house fan, the annoying hum of the refrigerator. Willing them to come back on.

Early afternoon on the next day, there was a *click*, and the hum was back. After fifty-two hours without power, just like that, life was normal again. But as I took my first shower in three days, it occurred to me that what the power outage on the Amtrak train had started—dealing with no running water or working toilets—the days in my house with no water/no flushes had finished. My days as a fussy germophobe were pretty much over.

And once I'd cleaned up the cluttered kitchen, our power-less days seemed like a bad dream. "If you've got to have one big storm of the season," John commented, "it's good to get it over with by mid-November."

I got back to my work project, and the week flew by. Then suddenly, it was Thanksgiving, and our day with my daughters and their families at Carrie's house. Seeing my grandchildren's sweet faces, I was filled with not only turkey and pie, but contentment—and thought how different this holiday was from last year's. There was no mess to embrace (save for that generated by a couple of little kids), or raised voices (save for the occasional fussing from Meghann's baby). Despite this quiet, orderly gathering, I somehow found myself missing Mom's sure-to-be lovingly disorganized dinner…I guess once a Boomeranger, always a Boomeranger.

After we cleaned up, Carrie offered us a bed for the night. But John and I regretfully declined, thinking of the next day's travel—we'd rather jump into a pool of piranhas than face "Black Friday," post-Thanksgiving shopping traffic. So we headed back home, looking forward to a blissed-out, Berryridge holiday weekend.

Then it started to snow.

74 ❦ Winter Wonderland

November might be Crazy Weather Month, but even back in town, the White Stuff this time of the year wasn't unheard

of. By Saturday evening, we'd gotten a decent little accumulation…
and the snow kept coming. And coming. Sunday, we awakened to a
whole new world of white—lovely, pristine, but far more snow than
you'd want to see when you live a mile from the main road. Judging
from the pile that had buried my car, it looked like about fourteen
inches.

Then the mercury began to drop. John pulled our tomato thermometer out of the snow, brushed it off, and parked it in front of the
kitchen window. The dial had dipped below twenty.

That night, I was roused by a strange, muted roar—like a jet flying
low overhead, or freight train rumbling past. Only planes can't hover
continuously in one spot…and we were fifteen miles from any train
tracks. Monday morning, our bedside clock was ominously dark,
no friendly red numbers showing a new day, with that odd, keening
sound growing louder. I peeked out of the bedroom window, and sure
enough, the skies were clear, with the trees bent over, tops pointing
southwest. Another winter Northeaster had arrived.

This wasn't the baby Northeaster we'd had a month ago. This was
the real McCoy. The Mother of all Northeasters. And up on our
ridge, surrounded by low mountains that funnel that fierce prairie
wind straight at us, Berryridge Farm received the full brunt of it.
But staying inside all day wasn't part of the program. I suited up to
fetch a box of wood, slogging through the drifts to the shed, only
to discover more of the Northeaster's mischief. Our woodshed was
full of snow.

On the coldest day we'd ever experienced, and with no power, our
small firewood supply was not only green, but wet.

John, you understand, keeps three grades of long johns.

He's got the light polypropylene kind, for indoors, then cotton
waffle "longies," as my dad called them, for "normal" winter weather.
And for extremes, John pulls out the Arctic class. Clearly, the man
knows how to dress for the cold.

A good thing, because while I was out getting wood, John remembered Garrett's advice about turning off the well-pump breaker.
Pulling on his high-top boots from his police days, he trundled out
to the pumphouse. He wanted to make sure that when the power was

restored, in the event ice had developed in the waterlines, the pump would stay offline until the lines were clear. Then he set up our little propane camp stove in the middle of the pumphouse floor, and put the flame on low. With luck, we had enough propane to keep the small structure warm enough so that the lines wouldn't freeze.

As the Northeaster gained strength, the wind howled, and the temperature dropped hourly, until it had sunk into the teens. The cold weather we thought we wouldn't be facing until January had not only arrived prematurely, but was far more extreme than we ever would have guessed. And we still had no power. Just like the outage twelve days before, all we had for water was what was left in the pumphouse tank—and without a working phone, we were again caught unawares.

Only this time, we weren't warm.

Our stove was working overtime, but inside the house you could practically see your breath. John had already donned his waffle johns, with a pair of Swiss army wool pants on top. We hovered around the woodstove, staring outside as the frigid, blasting wind sculpted the most curious snowdrifts around the house. A couple of cubic yards of snow hung off the edge of the roof, curling over so that it almost reached the snow on the ground. This hanging drift seemed to defy the laws of gravity—but then, in this other-worldly environment we found ourselves in, *everything* seemed different.

Whatever the weather, though, my routine includes getting out in it. I pulled on my seen-better-days, polypropylene johnnies, along with about four other layers of gear, boots with three pairs of socks, and ventured into the snow.

I got as far as the end of the driveway and had to stop; blocking it was a yard-high, twenty foot-long snowdrift. Taking a deep breath, I stomped though the drift with giant steps—kind of like when you're a kid playing "Simon Says." I figured I'd walk the mile down to the main road and check out the driving conditions. But I encountered more three-foot snowdrifts piled across our private drive. About a fourth of a mile from the main road, I came upon a fifty-yard stretch of high drifts. I tried to traverse it with more giant "Simon Says" steps. But for all my determination, after a couple dozen feet, the drifts defeated me. I literally could not lift my legs out of the snow to take the next step. I had to turn around.

"I hate to tell you this," I told John when I got home, "But we're… um, trapped."

We were not only cozily snowbound, but completely blocked from the outside world.

Now life was all about survival. The outdoor temp, according to the tomato, was in the single digits. Though John kept the woodstove stoked, the house grew colder and colder. By nightfall, our bedroom could've doubled as a SubZero refrigerator. What wouldn't I have given to turn on our Congressman furnace.

But staying warm was turning out to be the least of our worries. Without electricity, our well pump was offline. And with our water supply quickly dwindling, we couldn't leave the faucets open to a dribble. Now that the house had grown so cold, we faced more potential for disaster. The water pipes, from the connections in the pumphouse, to the ones under the house, were in danger of freezing. This scenario could mean not only broken pipes, but the ruination of the entire water system—which to repair, could cost thousands.

And now that we were snowbound, with no chance of driving to the village for bottled water, the likelihood of running out of water completely was getting more real by the moment. Feeling helpless, I turned to John. "What are we going to do?"

"There's not a lot we can do," John said, his face creased with worry. "Except try to keep the house as warm as we can. And hope it'll keep the pipes from freezing."

As darkness fell, John made another decision—he would stay up all night to keep the woodstove going.

75 Little Cold House

Plucky Laura Ingalls, of "Little House" fame, was my all-time favorite childhood heroine.

I'd read eagerly about her sturdy Midwestern pioneer family, with Pa, Ma, and the four Ingalls sisters overcoming many catastrophes: near-fatal illnesses, dangerous wild beasts like bears and panthers, even plagues of locusts. And scariest of all, cold weather. We're not talking about our near-zero degrees in the Foothills. But severe, terrible cold—like minus forty degrees. Or even minus fifty or sixty. Cold that would make cattle die from suffocation when their breath froze over their noses.

Out on the 1880's Dakota prairie, people like Laura's family often lived in homestead claim shanties with only tar paper for insulation. If you ran out of fuel during one of those cold spells, you froze to death. The Ingalls had known a family that had been forced to burn their furniture, but once that was gone, they all died. Another time, Laura was riding in a horse-drawn sleigh in something like fifty below. To be out in that cold makes you sleepy, so you've got to fight to stay awake. Because if you are so foolish as to drift off, thus slowing down your metabolism (in other words, your ability to keep warm), you can die. Even the best-case scenario is that your entire face will get frostbitten.

And as we all know from survival tales, at that point your nose turns black and falls off.

Those chilling tales weren't far from my mind that night, as John and I pulled the blankets off our bed and set up camp in the living room. The main drawback was that we had only one sleeping venue: our couch. Ever chivalrous, John offered, "I'll sleep on the floor."

"You will not," I chided him. "We can share." Keeping in mind that intimacy is good for a marriage, I curled up on one side, tucking my feet near John's chest. He did the same on the other end, his feet near my head. I'd heard author James Joyce and his wife Nora would often sleep head-to-toe to help limit the size of their family. But for us, the warmth more than compensated for the unorthodox sleeping arrangement.

Despite the cozy fire, I slept fitfully. My ever-faithful John took catnaps in between feeding the fire. When morning came, I unbundled myself from our nest of quilts to find we still had no power… and the tap no longer produced even a trickle. John's face was drawn with fatigue and worry about our water system. "If only we'd bought a generator," he said over and over.

Bundled up in our long johns and hats, we stayed warm enough through the chill hours, but our last pitcher of drinking water was almost empty. In true pioneer spirit, I couldn't succumb to the vapors. We did have a supply of water—and lots of it, just outside the door. I pulled out our turkey roasting pan, layered on my outdoor gear, then went out to pile mounds of snow in the pan. Back inside, I put the pan on top of the woodstove to melt.

Here's the thing, though. The snow surrounding your house may look pristine, but it isn't. When you heat with wood, no matter how highly EPA-rated your stove is, you'll find bits of ash not only inside your house, but all around your outside. And sure enough, the snow I brought in looked like I'd dashed it with pepper. Any water I'd end up with wouldn't do for drinking, but it would be just fine for everything else.

It was slow going, I can tell you. You know that truism, that it takes a foot of snow to equal an inch of rain? Well, translate that into usable water—you could mound that pan with enough snow to overflowing, and end up with barely enough liquid to cover the bottom. By dusk, my optimism was wearing thinner than fairy wings. Would we have to drink ash-flecked water? Or face another all-nighter with the woodstove?

Just as I was discovering how many roasting pans of snow you had to melt to get enough to flush your toilet, the microwave clock beeped, and the house fan came on. Power! Hallelujah!!

John hurried outside to turn on the well-pump breaker. Eager to wash my face, and even more, to flush, I still had to wait—the pump would need some time to fill the pressure tank. Finally, I turned on the kitchen tap.

Zip.

I tried the bathroom faucets. But still nada. I tracked down Mr. Fix-it Junior. "Houston," I said, "We've got a problem."

To diagnose the illness, Dr. John once again donned his Level 3, Arctic-grade long johns and tromped through the drifts to our pump-house. Moments later, he was back with a report. The little camp stove had indeed run out of propane, with a sad result. Our water system, hardly a half a year old, had died young. Like that tragic family in Laura Ingalls' story, it had frozen to death.

Now that we had electricity, at least we could contact the outside world. So John put in another call to Yoda—I mean, Garrett—to divine a cure. Despite all the unluckiness, or dare I call it, unpreparedness of the last days, we had more good fortune. Our water expert was home.

Garrett, bless him, gave John step-by-step instructions to get our water system running again. The first step was getting our furnace back in action, so that the warm air in the ductwork under the house could warm the pipes—"run it a couple of hours at seventy-five degrees," Garrett suggested. While I enjoyed my first hot flashes since living at Mom's, John laced his boots back up, and with his notes safe in his pocket, returned to the pumphouse to apply some CPR.

By 8:30 that evening, John had worked his magic. Our water system, like Lazarus, rose from the dead.

76 ❧ Still Snowbound

Do you ever notice that as soon as you've solved one problem, another one crops up?

Sure, we had power and running water again. Only the continuing frigid weather meant we were going through firewood like a well-fed baby through diapers. And mostly unseasoned wood at that. I discovered a whole new level of woodstove mess-tolerance when John and I decided to quick-cure more firewood by bringing it inside. After protecting the floors with construction-grade plastic garbage bags, we brought in box after box of wood, heaping more on top of what we had in the gravel room. Then we created a second three log-high pile by the front door. This new stack completely blocked the entry, but heck, we never used the door anyway.

Our private road was still drifted over, but on day three of the Big Chill, with the prospect of dry wood, I was feeling like we were in the catbird's seat. Besides, we had plenty of food for the next few days. John seemed unusually quiet though. "Is something the matter?" I asked.

"I think we'd better look into getting the road plowed."

I blanched. How much did it cost to plow a mile of road? $300?

$500? We still had no neighbors living on our private drive—no one to share the expense with. John seemed to read my mind. "This snow isn't melting anytime soon. We could be stuck here for weeks."

"You're right," I admitted. Isolation was one thing, but did I want to give up eating to save a few hundred bucks?

But the money issue was moot. First, we didn't know anyone who had a snowplow. Second, if the conditions on the main road were anything like the snowdrifts I'd seen on our drive, no one could get through anyway.

John had run into our nearest neighbor—the one living amongst the fir glen—once or twice. Joe ran a logging outfit, and judging from the occasional growl of engines reverberating up the ridge, he had some heavy equipment. We wondered…could he do any snow removal?

As far as John could tell, Joe seemed like a nice enough guy. Feeling desperate, we scrabbled through our collection of contractor's business cards, then hit pay dirt. John got on the phone.

Joe, as it turned out, wasn't at work, but home. Apparently you don't get a lot of construction-type work when the ground is frozen as solid as a bodybuilder's biceps. John asked him if there was any chance he could clear the worst drifts off the road. Joe said, sure, he'd take a stab at it. He didn't have a snowplow, but apparently, if you can push dirt around with an excavator, you can push snow.

In no time, we heard the rumble of his big machine—and for all our love of quiet, it was as welcome as a Mozart symphony.

John hiked out a quarter mile to meet Joe with the checkbook. And our excavating hero wouldn't let John pay him—not one nickel. "We're neighbors," Joe told him. "And I was getting cabin fever."

It felt really uncomfortable, to be so beholden to a near-stranger. But there really *is* something different about country living. Sometimes you just have to depend on people. And allow yourself to owe them. Someday—and you hope it won't be too long—you can return the favor.

77 ❦ Hard-Learned Lessons

After being snowbound for five days, a trip to the village sounded more alluring than a night out on the town. John and I ventured out in the pickup to get our mail and scare up some canned vegetables. And in case we got *another* power outage, more propane to keep the camp stove going in the pumphouse. Seeing broken trees everywhere, we discovered a Northeaster was as destructive, if not more so, as the warmer, southerly storms. The cold and wind had snapped big hemlocks and Douglas firs as if they were pencils.

On the drive home, John and I gave ourselves a good talking to: we wouldn't be caught with our long johns down again. Disaster-preparedness would be our biggest priority. First thing, we created a power outage kit—a box with candles, a flashlight, and lots of batteries. John went online and ordered a generator for the pump-house—5,240 watts—then we put a non-electric rotary phone on our shopping list. Let the power outages come—we'd still have water, *and* a way to call the power company. Then we phoned our site prep electrician, and scheduled the installation of a built-in pumphouse heater.

God willing, we'd never have to face a frozen water system again.

The next day, John and I watched our tomato thermometer dial slowly move upward, from the low teens to the low twenties. And in spite of four more inches of snow, the power lines held. I have to admit, learning to cope on the fly has a way of speeding up the aging process—we felt not only days older, but years wiser.

Too bad wisdom, like perfect vision, comes after the fact. Just as our greenhorn innocence had been a casualty of the cold snap, so had the potted nursery shrubs we'd hoped to plant "soon." Our darling kiddies had turned from lively green to a crispy, shriveled brown— as dead as our pumphouse had been. It wasn't just the $100 down the drain—John and I were filled with remorse. Had they suffered much? What an awful way to go, trapped in pots as the Northeaster kills your chlorophyll and dries your sap, while your mom and dad forgot all about you and are sitting inside a warm house during your death-throes. "From here on out," I said resolutely to John, "I vote no more buying plants until we have a place for them."

With the crisis behind us, we could use our computers again—and I had many hours to go to finish my project. After all we'd been through, I could hardly remember what it was about, but I turned on my laptop anyway.

Remember that scene in the movie *Jerry Maguire*, where Tom Cruise is crouched in front of his computer, face bathed in the dim glow of the screen? "I wrote and wrote and wrote," says the voiceover. Well, that's exactly what I did—I couldn't let wind, snow, cold, or a couple of power outages stop me. Two solid days of work later, I actually made my month-end deadline.

Elated, I shared my triumph with John at dinner. To have finished such a sizeable project during this disaster-filled November felt like a huge accomplishment...especially for someone like me, whose career has often felt more like putt-putt golf than a hole-in-one.

Although John smiled, said all the right things, he seemed far away. (When he's quiet, I've learned that means he's either thinking really hard, or worried about something. Which is often the same thing.) "Something on your mind, Honey?"

John looked like he didn't want to answer, then finally he said, "I don't think we've got enough wood."

In my usual attitude of "Don't worry, be happy," I hadn't thought of that. First thing the next morning, John and I trooped out to the woodshed and stared at what was left after our near-week of Arctic temps. All the time we'd lived here—nearly eight months—and all we had to show for it was a few stacks of small damp birch logs, and the chunks of alder John had cut up earlier in the fall, also damp.

What *had* we been thinking? Building a garden instead of a wood supply? Here it was only November thirtieth, and we had at least three more months of cold to get through, plus a long chilly spring. What if we had another cold spell like the one we'd just endured? Or several of them, without an operating woodstove? And we got snowed in again?

We would be not only inconvenienced, but in Big Trouble.

78 🦋 Woodn't it be Loverly

We got on the phone again. This time to my brother Ty, "The Wood Guy."

Ty's the risk-loving brother who narrowly escaped a serious head injury, as well as almost falling to his death in Dad's Country Squire. Ty runs a tree removal business. He loves wood. He knows wood. And he knows where to get wood.

I left a message, holding my breath. Today was Friday. Ty was leaving for his annual winter getaway—seven weeks in Mexico. Were we too late? We didn't know anyone else who could sell us some firewood—and to take a chance buying from a stranger, who might try to dump green wood on a pair of greenhorns, seemed unwise. While John and I were keen to avoid the furniture-burning scenario of those poor homesteaders, we were running out of options.

Ty returned our call a half-hour before his departure time. "Can we buy some wood from you?" I asked. "Dry wood, I mean."

"I don't have any to spare," Ty said reluctantly. "But I do know this guy…"

He gave me the number of a fellow who'd helped him on some jobs, and said he'd give Steve the heads-up that we'd be contacting him. I gave my brother our best bon voyage, then John got in touch with Steve. Hanging up the phone, he seemed more relaxed than he had in days. Lad Luck, in the form of Ty, had come through for us. Again.

Just like gift horses, when you get unexpected blessings, you don't examine them too closely. This Steve did have a cord he could sell us—some of it, he told us, was mountain pine that had been cut three years ago and stashed in someone's house back in Montana. John and I didn't care if Steve's firewood sounded too good to be true…we'd burn it if it was as green as the hills of Ireland.

As our messy indoor woodpile caught my eye, I had to wonder… who keeps firewood inside their house for several *years*? Apparently some old lady Steve knew who liked really, really dry wood. Anyway, our new Wood Guy said he'd deliver it Sunday morning.

After John's success at wood procuring, the sun breaking through the clouds seemed like a good omen. We'd come through some hard times—storms and cold and a frozen water system and being snowbound—but soon, we'd have a full woodshed. Our problems would be behind us.

John, however, looked really worn out. Of the two of us, he's more prone to worry, and he'd shouldered the lion's share of the stress. He'd been the one to stay up all night feeding the fire only four nights ago. He'd been the one struggling in the cold to get the pumphouse operational again. He'd also feel far worse than I ever could, if we ran out of firewood, and we had to throw ourselves on Mom's mercy. For both of us, having to ask my mom to put us up *again* would be snatching defeat from the jaws of victory.

Like we couldn't hack even our first winter in the Foothills.

Looking at John's pale, tired features, I couldn't suppress my wifely concern. "Are you okay?" I asked him after breakfast.

One step ahead of me (as usual), John said, "What if Steve can't get up the hill with his trailer?"

Although our yard was still buried in snow, our private road was passable—but just barely. In a few places, including the hilly section, the wind and cold weather had polished the snow into a solid sheet of ice. What if our firewood guy, a stranger upon whom we were so dependent, drove all this way, only to be unable to make the last half-mile to our driveway?

I couldn't imagine what it would be like to hand-haul a cord of wood all that way—and I certainly didn't want to find out.

I'm the first to admit that my eternal optimism can be sort of a character flaw. When you approach any situation figuring that things are going to work out somehow, once in a while, you don't always do your legwork. Or as John would say, take care of business.

When something needs doing, John, with those sturdy Midwestern genes, can be pretty dogged—and today, he wouldn't let this weather get the better of him. So he'd make sure our load of wood made it to our house...by hand-clearing the ice off the road.

Shortly after noon, John set out on foot down the drive with a heavy flat-bottomed shovel. Three hours later, I walked down to see how he was doing.

I met him trudging back home, looking bushed, the shovel slung over one shoulder. "How'd it go?" I asked him.

"Well, I got 'er done," he said tiredly.

I took a look at the road. "Oh, John…" He'd chipped the ice to make two parallel tire tracks, for what looked to be nearly the length of a football field.

I held out my hand for the shovel. "How much do you think you cleared?"

"I'd say maybe seventy-five yards," John said, passing over the shovel. He actually let me carry it home—which tells you how worn out he was.

After a hearty dinner, I expected him to bounce back, but instead, he didn't look quite right. I couldn't help asking, "Are you, um… really all right?"

John hates to be fussed over, so I didn't really expect him to admit he was tired. He's more likely to joke, "Let's just say I'll sleep good tonight." Instead, he rubbed his sternum. "My chest hurts a little."

This is never good news from someone who's had a heart attack. Still, John had done all the right things to make sure he never had another one: diet, exercise, Lipitor…. Shaken, I managed to ask calmly, "How long has it been bothering you?"

"All afternoon," he admitted. "And maybe a little bit yesterday."

"Did you take your aspirin?" I asked, trying not to panic. "And a nitroglycerin pill?" If your ticker isn't tocking right, these double-whammy meds should take care of it.

John had. But the pain didn't subside. As the evening wore on, the ache in his chest grew worse. Around ten-thirty, John said the same thing he'd said that long-ago November evening, exactly six years and twenty days ago. "I think we'd better go to the hospital."

79 🦋 A Long Day's Journey into Night

Since someone in the middle of a heart attack is not in any condition to take the wheel, I was the designated driver. I carefully negotiated the deserted, icy roads, still dicey after the recent load of snow, and tried to keep John's spirits up…as well as my own.

If there's one advantage to bringing a middle-aged guy with chest pains into the emergency room, it's this: there's no wait. Despite the late hour, just like six years ago, in moments John had a bed, medical personnel swarming around him like ants on an anthill, plugging in IVs, the EKG gizmo, the heart/blood pressure thingy in a plastic box suspended above the bed. You know it's just a machine, but you can't take your eyes off the impersonal flashing numbers tracking the life force of your beloved.

I put on a brave face, but my usual sunny optimism had finally hit reality. I was defenseless against the guilt coming at me in waves. John was getting excellent medical care, but would he really be all right? Had I let him do too much, with the road-clearing project? (Not that I think I could have stopped him.) I should have helped; maybe he wouldn't have overdone it.

But I had one more worry that I wouldn't allow into full consciousness. Had we taken on too much? To live our dream in the Foothills?

Getting admitted to a hospital is a lot like building a house *and* riding Amtrak. If you're trying to slow down, you've come to the right place. Nearly three hours after we'd arrived, John had finally gotten officially checked in. As we entered his hospital room around 2:30 a.m., I had to wonder: didn't they have a spare room earlier? It's not like they discharged someone at 2 a.m., thereby creating space for a new patient.

Anyway, we got John comfy in his fashionable cotton gown, and I stretched out on the plastic fold-down Barcalounger. The tests on John's heart had been inconclusive, so the doctors had decided to keep him overnight and do an angiogram in the morning. This would be John's second—the procedure with the groin incision so they can inject dye into a big vein, to see if you've got any blockages in your heart.

A modern hospital is that most unique of places, where you spend all your time in bed but you're not allowed to sleep. With the nurses coming in every half-hour and turning on the lights, it was a long night for both us. By morning, the snail-paced hospital ops resulted in more waiting—John's angiogram got pushed to the afternoon's docket.

After he was wheeled into surgery, I passed the time in the brand-new cardiac waiting room. On a weekend, I had the place all to myself. It resembled the kind of library you might find in a mansion—lots of antique-style (but brand-new) wood furniture, polished to a high gloss, pristine books in glass cases, very posh. Still, I couldn't relax, and just wandered around the room, in between visits to the nurses' station for news. When you're feeling the stress of your husband being in heart surgery, peaceful surroundings only get you so far. But finally, around 3 o'clock, John was in recovery.

He was drowsy, but in good spirits. I'd like to say it was John's natural resilience, but of course everyone feels good on the drugs they give you. Anyway, seeing his faint smile, I felt my natural optimism bounce back.

By and by, the cardiologist appeared for the post-surgery consultation. He had great news—John had *not* had another heart attack. No need, then, for the more invasive angioplasty. The doctor figured the chest pain had been an esophageal spasm, something John had experienced a few years back. It's an ache and pressure that feels a whole lot like a heart attack.

The consult included a follow-up handout for post-surgical care: take it easy the rest of the weekend, keep the surgical site clean, etc., etc. Since an angiogram doesn't involve the pop-rivet involved in the angioplasty, you could even get up and walk around afterward. But one item on the handout was in bold type. **If the incision starts bleeding, call 911.** But this was familiar territory. Years ago, John had recovered from his angioplasty like a pro, so regrouping from today's angiogram would be a walk in the park. As soon as the Valium wore off enough so he could walk, we were outta there.

Our big scare had turned out to be a bust. Feeling relieved, reprieved, John and I climbed into the pickup. "What about the wood

Steve's bringing?" John asked on the way home. (His way of saying *I won't be able to unload it.*)

"I'll stack it in the shed," I told him. All that pickaxing I'd done would finally be good for something.

In the last six days, John and I had made it through a giant snowstorm, a power outage, a water system freeze, and being completely blocked from the outside world. And now, we'd made it through this heart attack scare. Hauling a little wood by myself would be nothing. At last, we were back in the driver's seat.

Even if it was the slow lane.

After a stop at the grocery store, and another cautious drive home, we settled John on the couch. I gave him strict orders to let me coddle him—he'd been told to rest, and rest he would. In a burst of energy, I scurried around happily, cooking dinner, cleaning up, playing nurse to John. Then around nine, he came back from a trip to the bathroom. "Uh, it's bleeding a little."

I didn't need to ask what "it" was. We both took a closer look at the incision. "It doesn't seem like much," I said. "But it's not..." I closed my mouth, unwilling to finish. *It's not supposed to bleed.*

I re-read the post-op handout, then we got out a fresh gauze pad, and John applied a little pressure. A half hour later, the bleeding still hadn't stopped. In fact, blood was seeping out faster. Soon, it was soaking the bandage. My heart in my throat, I said, "We'd better call 911."

80 ❧ Foothills Crisis

In the city, if you call 911, within moments, the Medic One vehicle pulls up to your house and paramedics are all over you like fleas. When you live far out in the country—an hour's drive to the hospital in good driving conditions—it's not until you face a real emergency that you realize you have no idea where the nearest medical personnel will come from.

"We'll send an aid car," the dispatcher said immediately. I felt my insides unclench a little, even if she couldn't say how long it would

take. I only knew it would be a *lot* longer than in the city—the fire
station ten miles away didn't have an in-house staff of paramedics or
an ambulance. But on the way, to look after John until the paramedics arrived, was a stopgap medical team to provide first aid: the local
fire department volunteers.

But could they make it up to our house? Except for the stretch
of hill John had cleared, our mile-long private road was still ice and
snow-covered. Our driveway was a drifted-over mess. Between
checking John's wound every couple of minutes only to see more
blood, and peering out the kitchen window, I was as jumpy as a bead
of water on a hot griddle. It seemed like forever since I'd called 911.
But in less than half an hour I saw two hefty four-wheel drive vehicles
in the driveway, one with a light bar. And in moments, there was a
knock on the gravel room door.

When you're in a panic, your memory isn't the greatest. Apparently
all the stress hormones flooding your brain and bloodstream wreak
havoc with your cognitive abilities. Also, in that kind of state you
often forget social niceties like finding out people's names, or really
seeing their faces. As the team trooped in, I think there were five or
six of them, one a woman, all of them middle-aged except for one
younger guy. They were kind. And calm. As I led them to the living
room, I silently blessed each and every one of them.

Two of the guys actually apologized for tracking snow onto the
new carpet. One fellow, a real sweetheart, seemed to be in charge. He
took John's blood pressure, and examined the wound. "It's bleeding
pretty good, isn't it?" he said matter-of-factly. While he didn't act
like it was a terribly big deal, I was glad Medic One would be here
soon. Especially when our first aid crew didn't want John to move
off the couch. Or move much at all.

As we waited, the volunteers milled around, chatting with us and
each other. Then they got a call. The paramedics were phoning from
below, on the main road. They didn't think they could make it to
our house. Could the volunteers pack John in one of their vehicles
and bring him down?

Out went two or three of them to get the gurney. But since our
gravel room entry was so small, they'd have to bring the gurney in

through the front door—the one we *never* used. And the one blocked
by a pile of drying wood. As the guys dragged the gurney through
the front-yard snowdrifts, I shoved the wood out of the way and got
the door open just as they reached the steps. Within moments, the
team set up the gurney and positioned themselves around John—two
at his head, two at his feet, and one or two at his middle. With a
"One, two, three, LIFT," they got him onto the gurney and strapped
him in.

"He'll be all right," a couple of them said. "The guys down below
will take good care of him." Holding John's hand as they rolled him
to the front door, I kissed him goodbye, and thanked the crew. Then
I watched as they yanked that gurney with John's near two hundred
pounds through the path they'd broken.

As they rounded the corner, I ran to the kitchen window to see
the crew load John into the rig with the light bar. With tears in my
eyes and an ache in my throat, I didn't move until the revolving red
light disappeared from view.

A few minutes later our phone rang. The Medic One guys decided
they'd better take John in. That is, to the hospital. An hour's drive
away.

Although John was safe in the hands of professionals, I couldn't
help blaming myself. I should have insisted that he rest longer after
the angiogram this afternoon. And it had been my idea to go grocery
shopping after we left the hospital. Had walking around at the store
put too much pressure on his incision?

When you're stressed out, doing something active not only helps
take your mind off your troubles, but according to the medicos,
actually metabolizes your cortisol and adrenaline faster than if you
just sat around wringing your hands. So I fought my worry by doing
little things. Dishes. Cleaning the snow and dirt my fire department
angels had tracked in. Picking up stray wood bits around our hastily-
moved woodpile. Then from the kitchen window, I saw a sight that
stopped my blood cold.

A large vehicle with a light bar was crawling up our driveway. The
fire department volunteers' rig. But John was supposed to be on his
way to the hospital. What had gone wrong?

81 ❦ Aftermath

I watched, my veins feeling frozen, as a group of men unloaded the gurney with someone on it. Of course that someone was John. But why, why, why had they come back? As the volunteers plunged back into the snowdrifts with the gurney, I died a thousand deaths.

I could think of only one, terrible reason they'd returned so fast. Dear God, had John started hemorrhaging on the way down, or in the aid car, and they hadn't been able to stop it? And now they were bringing him back. Or rather, bringing his body back. Oh God, I prayed. Please don't let this happen. It can't happen. It's only a small incision. And we've only been married twelve years. I'm supposed to have another thirty or forty with him!

Once you hit middle age, you learn about death. I'd already watched my father draw his last breaths, sat with John's dad right after he'd passed. You've found out what death looks like. What it feels like. But you're not ready, you'll never be ready to lose your husband. Especially when you saw him only moments ago, full of life.

I tore the front door open, the frigid air surrounding me as the men struggled to lift the gurney. As they brought it into the doorway, John lifted his head, and smiled weakly. "They decided I didn't need to go to the hospital after all."

Then I did cry. Not huge shoulder-shaking sobs—I rarely weep, and not like that, not in front of people. But I didn't try to blink away the tears rolling down my face. It was all I could do not to drape myself over the crew and gurney in gratitude.

Breathless from exertion, our intrepid volunteers brought John into the living room, unstrapped him, then with another "One, Two, Three, LIFT," they heaved him back onto the couch. I hardly remember the rest. Didn't catch much of the paramedics reasoning behind forgoing the hospital. Who cared? John was okay, thanks to these half-dozen folks I'd never seen before.

Depending on the kindness of strangers is not just for Blanche DuBois.

The guys apologized again for tracking in more snow. "That's okay," I said. "I really, *really* don't mind." They could have tracked snow and dirt and whatever they wanted all over our blond bombshell carpet all night long and I would have welcomed it. Once the volunteers had John settled, with a few more precautions and jokes, they headed for the door. As I held it open, I thanked the team again and again, wishing it was socially acceptable to throw my arms around them. At that moment, I loved each and every one of them.

I loved them, and I didn't even know their names.

The aftermath of panic—that is, when the outcome is positive—is a joyful time. You laugh shakily, talk about what happened as if you'd ever forget the details, and some part of you knows that what you've just been through has changed you. Forever.

And you dimly realize what really matters. I did, anyway. Here on Berryridge Farm, where John and I had begun our new lives, it's the basics. Not money or fame. Not career aspirations. You've somehow learned that simply being together, getting food on the table, and staying warm is what counts. That, and being grateful. Forever.

Epilogue

I left the woods for the same reason I went there. Perhaps it seemed to me that I had several more lives to live, and could not spare any more time for that one... —Henry David Thoreau

As I write this, it's the one-year anniversary of that cold winter night. Like Thoreau, we tried out a new kind of life. But unlike him, John and I didn't leave the woods. If we have more lives to live, we're going to live them right here on Berryridge Farm.

True, it's not a farm, it's not even a farmette, but it's the dream of a farm. In spite of the bad weather and John's health scare, we knew in our hearts that we were meant to keep going. After all, we've barely scratched the surface of all the possibilities of our still-untamed acres.

Given our big plans, John and I face the never-ending challenge of establishing our place on a shoestring. Every so often, thinking of our lack of capital, John will talk about getting a part-time job. I'll say, "Honey, you know we'll make this work somehow," but he'll still look skeptical. Then something caught my eye in the newspaper that silenced this job notion for good.

"Look at this," I said to John, and showed him an article about the perks of working for a top mega-Internet company. "You're in a beautiful new high-rise in the middle of Seattle, you can take breaks in a game room that's open 24/7, and when the stress gets to you, there's in-house massage therapy. You can even get three catered meals a day—all free."

John snorted. "I'd rather live like Daniel Boone—catch a rabbit, skin it, put it on a stick and roast it over an open fire."

I think I would too...which pretty much says it all about our Foothills' mindset. Besides, John's labor is needed in-house—especially as we keep moving toward a nature-friendly, "keeping it local" way of running our little homestead.

We stopped burning our brush and wood junk, and now we toss it over the ridge into the monster slash pile Garrett created. It's starting to resemble the wall of thorns surrounding Sleeping Beauty's castle in the Disney movie. I wouldn't be surprised if another season's worth of wood scraps will raise the pile to level with the rest of the yard.

Once we realized that heating with wood meant our existence would narrow to a laser-beam focus—year-round firewood acquisition—John embarked on wood hauling and chopping and splitting with all the zeal of a sword-training Samurai. "It's better than going to the gym," he says. "Cheaper too."

Wising up about my priorities, I cancelled my subscription to the fluffo paper. Its East Coast focus was starting to seem not only long-distance, but out of another world. Then I decided to get on board with country living in earnest. I packed away my Pūr water filter and started drinking our on-site, unadulterated water. For one thing, I learned the filter is made in Mexico—which, like the newspaper, is not exactly local. And once you're ready to give up control over dirt, germs and orange floaty things, being persnickety about your tap water is a lot like washing your Foothills car. There's just no point.

About the same time my greenie-guilt about throwing out a quart of kitchen scraps every day hit critical mass, I also let go of worrying about bears. Thus began our move into true natural gardening: composting. Over time, our pile has become more of a compost *complex*, like condos, with building (pile) A, B, C, etc. I think we're now up to pile F. I'm happy to report that our complex hasn't attracted any wild critters, but if that time ever comes, I'll just move my compost operation out to the back forty. All the same, composting is like food-growing—a learn-as-you-go process. Tip for woodland composters: it's better to remove the rotten logs on your compost site *before* you've got three feet of compost on top of them, instead of *after*.

All my life, I labored under the delusion that life followed a certain predictable pattern. Long stretches of tranquility, punctuated by once-in-a-while incidents (from minor inconveniences to major upheavals), then things would go back to the way they were. But with the topsy-turvy years before we moved to the Foothills, and the months that followed in our new place, I finally saw that peace was fleeting—it was change that was constant.

Whatever happens, Albert Einstein said there are only two ways to live: as if everything is a miracle...or as if nothing is. It's like the way young children see the world, full of endless wonder. I like to think being open to a little mystery or synchronicity here and there guided John and me through our hard times. And I'm sure it helped us solve the puzzle of our Berryridge paranormal noise.

It turned out to be "nighthawks," as they're known in the Foothills. They're not hawks at all, but killdeer. At dusk, they fly at high altitudes, hunting for airborne treats, I imagine, with a most curious flight pattern. They'll make a sudden dive-bomb, then in a burst of exuberance, shoot skyward again—a split-second swoop that produces the distinctive, electronic *twang*—covering vast amounts of airspace that would never be available in the city. The real mystery is that the sound seems nowhere near the bird. Nature's ventriloquism, maybe, but it seems like one of those everyday miracles.

Eating food you've grown yourself feels like another one. When you're putting up fresh-picked, untouched-by-chemicals strawberries from your garden, you're enveloped by the sweet, heady aroma of ripe berries. And though your hands are sticky and red-stained, you're almost reluctant to wash the juice and heavenly scent off your skin. After you've stemmed your last berry, and finally get a chance to sit down with a bowlful...well, that's what I call magical.

When you think about it, your hopes and dreams and aspirations are ordinary miracles too...only it's up to you whether they wither away or take flight. I don't want to go all Zen on you or anything, but if there's one thing I can say about making dreams happen, it's this: Don't wait.

Don't wait until you have more money or more time or more flexibility. Don't wait until all the stars align. If you've got a dream burning inside you, there's a reason for it. So go ahead. Honor it.

Take the first, scary step and make it happen.

John and I discovered that our passion, to live a more engaged life, closer to the land, helps us feel grounded in a speeded-up, turbulent world. Sure, you don't get many chances to put your feet up, or sit under the grape arbor, drinking tea and communing with the bumble-bees. But you know what's really amazing about the slow life?

Time has never gone by so fast.

Suggested Reading and Resources

Also see our Web site: www.littlefarminthefoothills.com

Ivanko, John, and Kivirist, Lisa. *Rural Renaissance: Renewing the Quest for the Good Life* (Gabriola Island, British Columbia: New Society Publishers, 2004). www.ruralrenaissance.org

Kingsolver, Barbara, et al. *Animal, Vegetable, Miracle: A Year of Food Life* (New York: HarperCollins Publishers, 2007). www.animalvegetablemiracle.com

Muller, Wayne. *Sabbath: Restoring the Sacred Rhythm of Rest* (New York: Bantam Books, 1999). www.waynemuller.com

Pollan, Michael. *In Defense of Food: An Eater's Manifesto* (New York: The Penguin Press, 2008). www.michaelpollan.com

Thorpe, Gary. *Sweeping Changes: Discovering the Joy of Zen in Everyday Tasks* (New York: Walker & Company, 2000).

Sustainable Connections
1701 Ellis Street, Suite 221
Bellingham, WA 98225
www.sustainableconnections.org

Cloud Mountain Farm
6906 Goodwin Road
Everson, WA 98247
www.cloudmountainfarm.com

Countryside & Small Stock Journal
145 Industrial Drive
Medford, WI 54451
www.countrysidemag.com

About the Authors

Susan Colleen Browne is a graduate of Huxley College of Environmental Studies, Western Washington University. After several years in the environmental policy arena (and a couple of detour jobs), she turned her attention to writing and freelance manuscript editing. Her articles and columns have appeared in numerous newspapers and magazines; Susan is also a novelist and creative writing instructor, and is a frequent speaker and workshop leader at community colleges and writer's conferences. Her next book is a novel set in Ireland, *It Only Takes Once*.

When not writing, Susan is Berryridge Farm's chief cook and compost manager.

John F. Browne graduated from Western Washington University with a bachelor's degree in Fine Arts. He's a retired police sergeant; a former student of Akido, he taught personal safety classes and CPR for WWU's extension program. The owner of a small graphic design and photography business, John spends most of his time around trees: cutting firewood and nurturing the Berryridge orchard.